Dyslexia in the Primary Classroom

Wendy Hall

LearningMatters

Acknowledgements
The Author wishes to thank Stephanie Hall for providing the artwork in this book.

First published in 2009 by Learning Matters Ltd

© 2009 Wendy Hall

British Library Cataloguing in Publication Data
A CIP record for this book is available from the British Library.

ISBN: 978 1 84445 189 0

Cover design by Topics – The Creative Partnership
Project management by Deer Park Productions, Tavistock
Typeset by PDQ Typesetting, Newcastle under Lyme
Printed and bound in Great Britain by Bell & Bain Ltd, Glasgow

Learning Matters Ltd
33 Southernhay East
Exeter EX1 1NX
Tel: 01392 215560
info@learningmatters.co.uk
www.learningmatters.co.uk

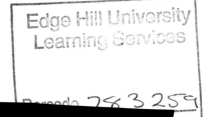

Contents

The Author

Currently employed at Liverpool Hope University as a senior lecturer in teacher training, Wendy has spent the past 20 years gaining qualifications in various aspects of special needs. Having qualified as a specialist tutor for dyslexia she taught privately in schools as well as providing special expertise on teacher training programmes.

Introduction

This text is written in the hope that more trainee teachers and newly qualified teachers will feel confident to observe children and note those they feel may not be developing in line with expected known norms. Ofsted (1999) noted in its findings that *pupils undoubtedly benefited where all the teachers had received awareness training about the nature and the implications of specific learning difficulties*. This book sets out to raise your awareness of specific learning difficulties (dyslexia) in order that you can better identify the child who may be at risk and address their needs through a variety of techniques including games. It is essential that children experiencing difficulties are spotted and have their difficulties addressed as soon as possible so that they can benefit from their time in school. This imperative was recognised in the House of Lords Dyslexia Debate in December 2005 when Lord Laird noted: *It is not simply a matter of having a specialist teacher. There has to be a far wider understanding among all teachers of the problems that children may face in reading and writing.* Baroness Walmsley furthers this when she states: *Initial Teacher Training (ITT) needs to be changed urgently if Every Child Matters is to be seen as more than just rhetoric. The absence of sufficient dyslexia and Special Educational Needs (SEN) tuition within ITT has been a cause for concern for many years.*

This book outlines practical activities and illustrates the use of games as a tool for teaching children when other methods may have failed or will not engage the children. It has been at the request of many trainee teachers that I have put together this text outlining many of the games which I have used in teaching children and which have enthused both the children and trainees teachers (as well as some experienced teachers).

I owe a great debt of gratitude to those trainees for pushing me into writing this book. It is hoped that it will prompt your own creativity and provide you with the rationale and confidence to create your own games.

Some of the chapters are heavily theoretical and I make no apologies for this. You have to know the theory behind an activity to know how and why to adapt it, in order to evaluate its impact. You need to know why you are undertaking a certain course of action. I believe it is this lack of theoretical underpinning of play which has eroded the place of play and the value of learning by investigation and enquiry. Thankfully this is now returning to our classrooms but you still need to know why. You still need to understand the rationale for why play works and how children are motivated.

As a trainee and a newly qualified teacher it is your responsibility to provide for the needs of all of the children in your class, not just those who are easy to teach. It is your responsibility to know how to proceed and seek more help if necessary, how to refer on at the appropriate time. I hope that when you have used this book you will feel confident to do this.

It is not intended that you read this book from front to back. It is a resource book; however, you probably do need to read the first few chapters to start with at least so that you get an idea of the complexity of the most common classroom learning difficulty and what the signs and symptoms are. After that it is important that you refer to the chapters appropriate to the needs of you and your children.

I hope you will find the book useful. Feel free to adapt the games to your needs and to the interest and ability level of the children. They are not set in stone or sacrosanct. The art of creativity is using the ideas of others and making them your own and coming up with another original idea. If you do this then I have succeeded in my aim.

REFERENCES REFERENCES **REFERENCES** REFERENCES **REFERENCES** REFERENCES

Ofsted (1999) *Pupils with specific learning difficulties in mainstream schools*. London: HMSO

Report on House of Lords Dyslexia Debate 7 December 2005 accessible at BDA: www.bdadyslexia. org.uk/downloads/Lords.pdf (accessed 15/9/08)

1
What is dyslexia?
Causes and consequences

Chapter objectives

By the end of this chapter you should be aware of:

- **the main theories of causation of specific learning difficulty (dyslexia) (SpLD [dyslexia]);**
- **the different theories surrounding SpLD (dyslexia) and how they impact on responses to dyslexia;**
- **a variety of response theories to SpLD (dyslexia).**

This chapter addresses the following Professional Standards for QTS:

Q1, Q3(a), Q5, Q19, Q26(b).

Introduction

This chapter will examine the following.

- The nature of the complex of disabilities commonly known as dyslexia.
- The causes of dyslexia.
- The main theories pertaining to this condition.
- What the consequences are in terms of learning disability.
- Other issues such as teaching methods.
- The impact on family and friends.

Often the socialisation of children with dyslexia is different to that of other children in the class and their families because they are embarrassed by their dyslexia and need to preserve self-esteem as much as possible. All of these are consequences but often the focus is only on the learning outcomes.

Theoretical background

Terminology

Specific learning difficulty (dyslexia) is not a new condition although the terminology of it has changed somewhat over time. 'Specific learning difficulty' has only recently been adopted and this reflects the fact that the condition is specific to the person, specific in its symptoms to that person: it is a learning difficulty, not a generalised disability. The 'dyslexia' appendix is added to denote this umbrella term rather than dyspraxia, which is also a specific learning difficulty. However, as you will see, dyslexia itself can present in different forms and subgroups; it is not a homogenous group or consistent in its presentation, although the clustering of symptoms forming the syndrome is reasonably predictable to an experienced dyslexia tutor. *Developmental* dyslexia is most common in children, *acquired* dyslexia is more common in teenagers and adults as a result of trauma to the brain. As the name suggests, this type of dyslexia is acquired once language has developed normally. Developmental dyslexia is present from very early on, often detectable in retrospect from the moment the child starts to develop oral language.

Some history of dyslexia

The newcomer to dyslexia would be forgiven for thinking that dyslexia is a relatively new phenomenon; however this is clearly not the case. A comprehensive history beyond the scope of this chapter is presented by Ott (1997). She cites Critchley (1996) as outlining the description of dyslexia given in 1672 by Thomas Willis, which predates the usually named source of Professor Berlin in 1887. Kussmaul is cited in Ott (1997) identifying word-blindness in stroke victims while Hinshelwood is credited with work on patients who while still retaining the ability to work with numbers lost the ability to read words. The late 1800s provide evidence of many professionals identifying the symptoms of dyslexia or word-blindness. These include William Pringle in 1898 and in the same year James Kerr. Orton's work in 1952 is probably the most famous noted while in 1956 Anna Gillingham and Bessie Stillman, as a result of work carried out by Orton, devised the multisensory approach which prevails and has influenced today's methods of teaching dyslexic people. Miles (1996) applauds the work undertaken at Aston University which resulted in the Aston index – a predictive and descriptive instrument for identifying the dyslexic patterns of difficulty and which can be used by the class teacher. Growth in understanding in the UK has been steady throughout the 1950s to 1972 when the British Dyslexia Association was founded (Ott, 1997) The Dyslexia Institute has since been founded along with the Hornsby International Institute, with the two organisations merging in 2005 to become DyslexiaAction. You can see then that dyslexia has been recognised for the difficulties it presents for a long time even though formal acknowledgement of it as a 'real' phenomenon is only relatively recent.

Disability or special educational need?

It is worthwhile at this point to consider what a disability is and how this might be different from a child with special educational needs. Many people would not consider something such as dyslexia to be a disability because it cannot be seen. Indeed this is where much of the prejudice towards dyslexia has evolved from, with the perception that people with these difficulties typical of dyslexia are lazy or stupid or that it is just the excuse of many parents as to why their children fail in literacy skills.

The Equalities and Human Rights Commission (EHRC) website records anyone who has a disability as someone who has:

> a physical or mental impairment which has a substantial and long-term adverse effect on his ability to carry out normal day-to-day activities.

Learning is classified as one of those day-to-day activities.

A child with a special educational need is one who has a learning difficulty which calls for special educational provision to be made for them. Section 1 of the Code of Practice (DfES, 2001) provides a good outline of how the two categories may overlap or be totally different. It outlines how a child with a special need may have significantly greater difficulty than their peers. However, the greatest distinguishing feature between the two is that a special educational need may be temporary; indeed many children with special educational needs receive temporary help which puts them on the right path and they then maintain progress with their peers. This is the aim of special needs support and of the programme of Reading Recovery which has been government-funded in recent years – to return the child to their rightful position along with their peers. A disability is something which you have for at least 12 months (the only exceptions to this are terminal illnesses which are counted from the diagnosis). Furthermore, the EHRC site notes that not all children with a disability will have an SEN: some medical conditions such as asthma or visual impairment may be classified as a disability but not result in a child needing SEN support. A very able child who is dyslexic may be classified as having a disability (if it affects their everyday life) but may not be in need of SEN support because they are not falling behind their peers in school and therefore not included under the Code of Practice definitions as in need of SEN resources.

The EHRC further indicates that it is illegal for schools to discriminate against a person with a disability through: *Admissions and in the curriculum either through teaching or resources.* However, to monitor and enforce this is almost impossible unless parents can make a case for their child.

PRACTICAL TASK PRACTICAL TASK PRACTICAL TASK PRACTICAL TASK PRACTICAL TASK

Make a list of all of the types of communication that might be considered under the EHRC guidance. Consider how you would provide an alternative means of access.

You will need to consider not just the child but also parents, carers and guardians.

Make a comprehensive list of the resources available and how you might adapt or modify them to make them more accessible.

A recent case has established that there can also be discrimination by association. This is likely to be a landmark case. Gillhooly (*TES*, 2008) reports that the European Court of Justice upheld a previous ruling, by the Advocate General in England, that allows that disability discrimination is not limited to just the person with the disability but can extend to those associated with the person with the disability. This has implications for children whose parents are dyslexic and are unable to support them in their literacy development. The school needs to support them if it is known that the parents cannot. However, this is an examination beyond the scope of this book.

The Code of Practice (DfES, 2001) (CoP) outlines various areas which are impacted by learning difficulties and even outlines specific learning difficulties (dyslexia) (SpLD (dyslexia)) specifically. SpLD (dyslexia) therefore can rightly be called a disability and in most cases a special educational need; however, the extent to which it is allowed to interfere with a person's everyday life is within our control. There are some people with SpLD (dyslexia) who are minimally affected (and in fact are often undiagnosed). However, around 5% are severely affected and it is this group where most influence can be exerted. The nomenclature of SpLD (dyslexia) is rather wordy and can cause confusion for some people thinking that it is different from the condition commonly known as dyslexia. There are also some people who feel they would rather not be termed 'disabled' – they have a learning difficulty which is open to being addressed if the appropriate measures are taken. For these reasons this text will now use the more commonly known and understood term of dyslexia.

Dyslexia is context-bound and socially constructed in as much as societies which place little emphasis on literacy would not consider the difficulties to be of great importance. There is also some evidence to suggest that the incidence of dyslexia is greater in societies that use an alphabetic system rather than logographic or ideographic systems. It is perfectly possible for a pupil to be dyslexic in one language but not in another. That is not to say that the underlying difficulties which affect dyslexic people are not present in those societies and languages; indeed studies of Chinese children found that there was an incidence of difficulty with phonic assimilation and synthesis but the impact this had on learning the language was less because Chinese is not an alphabetic language. However, as Smythe (2008) points out, you are likely to be teaching children through the language of English and may encounter dyslexic children who display dyslexia through the medium of English. This is of prime concern to you.

So the difficulties which are part of dyslexia can be found worldwide even if the full condition of dyslexia is not recognised although the signs have been noted through time from 1672 to the present day.

Definitions

Dyslexia was first recognised and noted by the medical profession and thus medical defini-tions prevailed. A medical model of dyslexia prevailed with dyslexia being a deficiency in the biological system to be corrected if possible through the medical profession. Once educa-tionalists started noting the difficulties of dyslexic children, educational definitions started to be given credence. This gave rise to an educational model of remediation of these difficul-ties. More recent theories have placed dyslexia as a socially constructed condition. The social model holds prominence today, arguing that it is society which makes dyslexia a barrier in life rather than the condition *per se*, the analogy being with using a wheelchair. If you use a wheelchair and have an office upstairs, it is not the wheelchair but the stairs that are the barrier. Some would argue it is a combination of the two. So today we have the societal and educational models sitting side by side.

Models of dyslexia

Early definitions made the distinction between ability and performance and were exclusive models rather than inclusive models. If there were other reasons why a child might fail such as a disrupted family life or poor social conditions, these were reasons to rule out dyslexia as a cause of the difficulties.

One definition (Perfetti,1985), which is representative of many, indicates that to be consid-ered dyslexic rather than just a poor reader the child should be at least of normal IQ and two years behind in the reading achievements. The same source indicates that there should be no other reason which could explain such a discrepancy, including social, economic, moti-vational or emotional factors.

This type of definition with its focus on reading age lag is still predominant in supplying extra support in many Local Authorities (LAs) today and as will be seen later in this book can exclude many children who may be dyslexic but do not satisfy this one criterion. Ofsted (1999) found that where this criterion was applied and a child did meet it, often dyslexic children were grouped with other children who were also two years behind their chrono-logical age for reasons other than dyslexia, such as global learning difficulties. Grouping in this manner was criticised by Ofsted for placing otherwise able children in a lower-attaining group below their true ability level. Unfortunately some of our more recent government reports use this type of definition because there have been no really adequate ones to replace them.

Furthermore, it is not to say that children who do come from these groups (social or economic disadvantage, emotional factors, etc.) may not be dyslexic. Being part of these groups does not protect you from dyslexia and this is the danger of such definitions. Lowenstein (1996) cites Lowenstein (1989), who favours a more general definition of *children who have difficulty in learning to read for no apparent reason despite good verbal intelligence*. This definition again focuses on reading and the discrepancy with intelligence tests however Kelly (1998) disputes this, saying: *Historically dyslexics are differentiated from other poor readers on the basis of intelligence ... there is no empirical evidence for this assumption*

Furthermore, when different reading tests are compared, not only might they measure different aspects of reading such as word identification rather than comprehension, but it is now recognised that there may be a discrepancy in reliability between tests in the age at which they are rendered. It is possible to gain reading ages of two years' difference when a variety of reading tests are taken by a child on the same day. Reading age therefore is not a reliable indicator of a child's ability or even attainment at a particular point in time. More recently a new measure of success and ability is being used. Progress in Letters and Sounds is being used to group children as young as five years old (Ofsted, 2008). There is even evidence of some schools creating ability groups across year groups just for phonics lessons.

More recent definitions have taken a broader view and don't refer to other factors. However, the nature of these very broad definitions causes a difficulty just as much as the exclusionist ones.

The British Psychological Society (BPS, 1999) provides a very broad and not very helpful definition:

> *Dyslexia is evident when accurate fluent reading and or spelling develops incompletely or with great difficulty. This focuses on literacy learning at the word level and implies that the problem is severe and persistent despite appropriate learning opportunities. It provides the basis for a staged process of assessment through teaching.*

This is the definition used for the House of Lords Dyslexia Debate (2005). The definition is so general that it has drawn criticism from academics who state that it goes so far as to claim that the term 'dyslexia' has been over-generalised to refer to anything from straining one's eyes to read under adequate lighting to specific cerebral defects or damage associated with the inability to interpret symbols. However, this is the definition accepted by the present government and the one which drives resources. A more recent definition by a leading scholar in the area of dyslexia is provided by Reid (2004), who describes it as:

> *[A] processing difference experienced by people of all ages, often characterised by difficulties in literacy, it can affect other cognitive areas such as memory, speed of processing, time management, co-ordination and directional aspects. There may be visual and phonological difficulties and there is usually some discrepancy in performances in different areas of learning. It is important that the individual differences and learning styles are acknowledged since these will affect outcomes*

of assessment and learning. It is also important to consider the learning and work context as the nature of the difficulties associated with dyslexia may be more pronounced in some learning situations.

You will find further definitions at www.dyslexia-information.com including the definition adopted by the International Dyslexia Board, also used by the US National Institute of Child Health and Human Development (NICHD) (2002), which is:

Dyslexia is a specific learning disability that is neurological in origin. It is characterised by difficulties with accurate and/or fluent word recognition and by poor spelling and decoding abilities. These difficulties typically result from a deficit in the phonological component of language that is often unexpected in relation to other cognitive abilities and the provision of effective classroom instruction. Secondary consequences may include problems in reading comprehension and reduced reading experience that can impede growth of vocabulary and back-ground knowledge.

The definitions are often confusing, contradictory and unclear in the use of terminology. The quest for an adequate definition is important because, as Kelly (1998), states: *the situation reflects not only the perception of the user but the fundamental and long-standing disagreement about the nature of reading problems.*

You may be asking why it is important to have a good definition as long as we all know what to look for in children and be able to refer them on. A definition is very important for the following reason: the definition may determine the assessment and could exclude some children who may not meet the criteria in terms of reading but may have severe difficulty with spelling or writing.

Chia (1996) lists three reasons for such difficulty at arriving at a universally accepted definition of dyslexia:

The failure to locate stable correlates of dyslexia.
The lack of clarity in delineation of dyslexia often resulting in a poor understanding of the relationship between reading and language.
Too many terms, inclusive of the term dyslexia as well have been coined to describe this learning difficulty resulting in entanglement of synonyms.

(Chia, 1996, p33)

The whole process of using definitions is fraught with difficulties. However, for ease of use and in the absence of other more suitable ways of selecting 'at risk' children there is a danger of adopting an exclusive definition rather than an inclusive one, especially with regard to the notion of IQ and the criterion that a child should have a reading age two years behind chronological age. This is at odds with the Code of Practice, which indicates that a pupil who has significantly greater difficulty in learning than the majority of children of the same age is one who needs special educational support (DfES, 2001, p6); this is without a further requirement to meet an arbitrary criterion related to reading age. It may be that the child is in a class where all of the children are achieving above the national norm; the child with dyslexia may not be achieving at the same level or at the same rate as the rest of the class and may be hampered in their progress by dyslexia. However, because of the general level of ability in the class and that of the child they may not be two years behind their chronological age. Indeed the higher the IQ, the less likely this situation is, the IQ masking the dyslexia but also the dyslexia masking the IQ because of the reading difficulties. Nor should the possibility that a less intelligent child may be dyslexic be ignored. The difficulty here is to ascertain how many of the difficulties are a result of low intelligence and how many are due to dyslexia. The problem in many cases, especially compound cases, is apportioning cause to different contributory factors. It would appear therefore more helpful to turn to lists of behaviours and characteristics that would guide a teacher in identifying the pupils potentially at risk of dyslexia.

Whichever definition we subscribe to dyslexia can be outlined as something which is medical in origin, can be described by and is of concern to psychologists, and manifests itself in education and can be exacerbated by cultural mores and systems.

But what is this condition called dyslexia? Is your understanding of dyslexia the same as that of the person in the next room/school? It is crucial that if we are discussing a condition which is highly prevalent in classes we should share a common understanding of what we are talking about.

REFLECTIVE TASK

When dyslexia is mentioned, what do you perceive to be the profile of that person; what are their difficulties and what are their strengths? Take ten minutes to get a cup of coffee and note down your thoughts about what a dyslexic child can and cannot do.

Comment

- Did you include in the top few difficulties inability to read and bizarre spelling? While these are true of the majority of dyslexic people there is one subgroup of dyslexic people who are in fact very good decoders of print and good at learning spellings. (See 'Hyperlexia' later.)
- Did you mention difficulty in naming objects and difficulty with recall of words?
- Did you also mention lack of general organisation?
- Did you mention poor handwriting?
- Did you note difficulty with musical notation?
- Did you mention difficulty with all curriculum areas?
- Did you mention behaviour challenges? Often these other areas of the syndrome are aspects which are overlooked in the focus on spelling and reading.
- Did you note that some dyslexic people may have difficulty with phonics while some may be relatively good at phonics but may have huge difficulties with look and say systems of reading and spelling? More of this later.
- Do you perceive dyslexia to be a single group of characteristics and symptoms?

Subgroups

Dyslexia is a term used to describe an umbrella of signs and symptoms. However, not all dyslexic people will manifest all of these signs and each person's profile of strengths and weaknesses will be individual. Depending on the profile and the extent to which a person presents at either end of the spectrum, different tuition may be necessary. It would be totally inappropriate therefore to say all of these children are dyslexic and can be taught together as is the case in some schools. The most commonly identified subgroup is the dysphonetic group, which has difficulties with the sound-to-symbol correspondence of the English language. The second subgroup is the dyseidetic group, who can sound out words but has difficulty with remembering everyday words and extreme difficulty learning sight words even when these have been encountered on many occasions. Chia (1996) suggests that an examination of the spelling of the child will point to which subgroup they belong to. *Dysphonetic* children will misspell and use their visual memory skills to learn words but will have few strategies for spelling or reading unknown words. *Dyseidetic* children will use phonic skills to spell most words and most words will be readable if you say them exactly as they are spelt. They will misspell sight words, spelling them using their phonic skills. They will also over-apply the rules they have learnt. Chia puts forward the position that these two groups are actually at extreme ends of a continuum where, more commonly, most children lie somewhere between with strengths and weaknesses in different proportions. Suppositions have been put forward as to how these various subtypes reflect the different models of reading whether by the indirect route of phonics or the direct route of look and say. You will read more about the routes to reading in the chapter on supporting reading.

A third group, *hyperlexia*, may go undetected for some time. This group can learn spellings and sight words, can sound out non-words but has extreme difficulty remembering what they have read, will understand little of what they have read. They also have difficulty in constructing meaning so their written work may make little sense but what is written will often be spelt correctly.

You may also come across the terms 'deep dyslexia' and 'surface dyslexia'. A useful model for understanding the debates surrounding dyslexia is put forward by Chia (1996) and is termed the tri-continua model.

The exact terminology is not important at this stage for you to understand. What is important is that you recognise that dyslexia is not one 'condition' which is always the same. It varies from one individual to another in type and severity.

What is dyslexia and what are the causes?

To understand what dyslexia is, it is first essential to outline some of the theories and evidence around dyslexia in order to correctly place the symptoms within a paradigm. There are various theories about why dyslexia exists and what causes it. Below are some theories; however, as research into dyslexia progresses you may come across new theories which either support or challenge existing theories. The different theories can be categorised into the different domains from which they have evolved.

Cognitive theories

The phonological deficit hypothesis
This has been the dominant, and is still currently the most subscribed to, theory to explain dyslexia. It is argued that abnormalities around the area of the brain processing language (see below) lead to failure to develop phonological awareness and difficulties in processing phonology and interfere with the learning of phoneme-to-grapheme correspondences. This is supported by genetic research which indicates that differences in the brain structure interfere with learning because of genetic differences in those people. Certainly the majority of dyslexic groups tested for skills deficit fall into this category. However, it must be remembered that not all children with dyslexia have this deficit, as demonstrated by Chia.

Double deficit hypothesis
Lack of fluency in reading is hampered further by lack of processing speeds. Early testing of rapid naming in 1976 (Denckia and Rudel) showed that there were severe delays in naming pictures of colours in children with dyslexia against a normed sample. It has also been shown by Yap and Vanderleij (1993) that dyslexic children need longer exposure to words or letters in order to identify them.

The automatisation deficit theory
Nicolson and Fawcett in the early 1990s found that there was a commonality of some deficits in groups of dyslexic children, quite different from the individual profile usually found. This group of deficits includes lack of balance and poor motor skills as well as phonological deficits and rapid-processing deficits. Dore has recently claimed these are the main cause of dyslexia and has set up the Dyslexia Dyspraxia Attention Treatment Centre (DDAT) to remediate such deficits, according to a report broadcast on *Tonight* with Trevor MacDonald (Henry, 2002a). While new research and findings are always welcome, to make the claims that Dore did in 2002 gave false hope to many parents (Henry, 2002b). Dore claimed that dyslexia is caused by the impaired working in the cerebellum, which controls co-ordination and by paying attention to co-ordination and improving this aspect will essentially 'cure' pupils of their dyslexic symptoms.

Brain-level theories

Cerebral cortex hypothesis
Galaburda (1985, cited in Chia, 1996) has recorded evidence of differences in the brain structure of dyslexic people. This hypothesis links the language facility and the differences which are most marked in the part of the brain dealing with language and you will see that this links with the phonological deficit theory. Brain mapping continues and there are many observations about the differences between the brains of dyslexic and non-dyslexic people and how they process language. This includes work undertaken by geneticists examining how genes affect the brain and its functions.

Magnocellular deficit hypothesis or scotopic sensitivity syndrome/Irlen Syndrome
There is extensive evidence regarding the lack of stability and visual processing of some dyslexic people. Livingstone et al. (1991), Stein and Walsh (1997) concur that magnocellular pathways to the brain are implicated in the processing of information in the different parts of the brain. Irlen (1991) has identified difficulties with visual pathways causing difficulties with:

- background accommodation;
- light sensitivity;
- background accommodation;
- sustained attention;
- span of recognition;
- print resolution;
- depth perception/gross motor activities.

This gives rise to flicker movements of letters and words, splayed lines, reduced focus, blurred vision, lack of clarity of vision and often headaches.

There is still some debate about whether this is a separate condition from dyslexia or is a subgroup, as suggested by Ramus (2001), who states that this set of symptoms is applicable to a subset of dyslexic children. This would explain why research around coloured filters on a varied section of dyslexic people would result in mixed findings, with only some of the children benefitting.

Genetic explanations

There is now a clear indication of a genetic aspect. Research by Taipale et al. (2003) reported the link and importance of genetic studies and drew attention to diet as well as the fact that particular chromosomes are clearly identified with developmental dyslexia. This work in relation to genetic background was supported by the research of Schumacher et al. (2007) which indicates family mapping as highly predictive of the likelihood of learning disability. Neither study however looked at sex-specific linkage; there has been further reporting that this link is greater in boys than girls. Gruen is reported in *Bio-Medicine* to have carried out research which locates the difference in gene DCDC2 which is expressed in the reading area of the brain. He is reported as saying *this very architecture of the brain is necessary for normal reading*. The Open University course literature identifies that boys are more at risk from this than girls because boys have an XY chromosome whereas girls have a double X chromosome. Where there is a 'faulty' X chromosome girls have another one to compensate, whereas boys do not. There are also studies examining the role of testosterone in the developing foetus. A male child with one dyslexic parent has a 50% chance of being dyslexic; if this parent is the father the chances are greater. However, one danger of genetic research is the assumption of inevitability. This position reasons that because there is family history a child will inevitably have dyslexia. The other assumption is that because it is genetic there is little that can be done about it. It is not guaranteed that a dyslexic father (or mother) will pass on the 'dyslexic gene' to the son. And the brain does not develop solely on the basis of genetics. It develops as a result of interplay between environmental factors, stimulation of the brain as well as genetic factors. Nonetheless, it is something that teachers should be on the lookout for – a family history of dyslexia which at one time was dismissed as folklore.

Neurobiology of dyslexia

There is now substantial evidence from autopsies to indicate that the structure of the brain of known dyslexic people is different from that which may be expected from an examination of the rest of the population or what might be termed the 'normal' brain. This is especially true of boys. The following differences have been noted

- An uneven development, with the left hemisphere of the brain being underdeveloped with the concomitant overdevelopment of the right hemisphere (Galaburda, 1985, cited in Chia, 1996).
- Ectopias growing on the brain which are not typical of 'normal' brains.
- Connections between the two halves of the brain which are not typical of normal development.
- Greater development in parts of the brain controlling other creative features such as musical ability, artistic talent, etc.

Why would this be important? Curran (2008) outlines how the left hemisphere is dominant even in left-handed people and it is this hemisphere that deals with language, analytical and sequential processing while the right-hand side of the brain deals with non-verbal, holistic and parallel processing. In 'normal' brains the two hemispheres are more or less even and the connections between the two are mapped precisely, the two halves have to 'communicate quickly and efficiently with each other' in order to process information efficiently. Gruen's research, as outlined on the BBC website (2005), supports this proposition and was also published by an American online journal *Bio-Medicine* under the title 'Chromosome 6 has the dyslexia gene', also in 2005. The left hemisphere does not work alone but relies on the right-hand side and vice versa. Curran further explains how the mapping of nerve cell to nerve cell in an exact manner allows information to travel from one part of the brain to another and arrive 'uncorrupted'. In essence this does not happen in people with dyslexia because of the ectopias on the brain which prevent this exact mapping and which create extra neuron pathways, Curran (2008) adds that another specialised area of the left hemisphere is in dealing with mathematics while the right-hand side is involved in processing the incoming data from the left-hand side. He concludes: *so lateralisation of function is central to how your brain works.* It is easy to see how if the two halves have not developed in the expected way and the information pathways are not mapped in this precise way but 'corrupted', then it will be more difficult to learn, remember and process information.

This information is really only of importance in helping you understand that this is a genuine difficulty with many children; it is not 'put on', it is not an excuse for middle-class parents whose children are not learning to read, it is not a child just being lazy. There are very real difficulties which have real causes and real consequences. The consequences are the real matter for educationalists as it is in school that the signs of dyslexia are displayed most markedly and where unless there is an understanding and adaptation then the most damage can be done.

How learning is affected

Even though there is continuing debate as to whether the left-hand side of the brain has not developed adequately or whether the right-hand side has developed more than would be expected, what we can be sure of is that the right-hand side has started to undertake some of the activities normally associated with left-hemisphere function. This causes difficulty when we look at how other children (and brains) process language, particularly reading. This part is particularly relevant to the current thrust to teach all children through synthetic phonics, so read carefully here. There is a lot of evidence that the most efficient way of reading is the direct route: seeing a word and recognising it. For single-word recognition this would work relatively efficiently especially for irregular words such as 'yacht' and it is how most experienced, efficient and adult readers process information.

This can be shown diagrammatically thus:

PRINTED WORD → PRELIMINARY VISUAL ANALYSIS (RECOGNITION) → LEXICON → OUTPUT

The lexicon is informed and supported by the reader's knowledge of the semantic system.

The phonic or indirect route, which is more complex, has to bypass this system and works as follows:

PRINTED WORD → PRELIMINARY VISUAL ANALYSIS → GRAPHEME-TO-PHONEME CONVERSION → PHONEME BLEND → LEXICON → OUTPUT

As you can see, this is a much more complicated process and relies heavily on working memory.

Phonics (synthetic) is an indirect route and it requires the child to recognise the grapheme, process it in the brain, assign a phoneme to it and produce that sound, then to combine sounds. The brain has to do this twice over and synthesise the two sounds (or three or four sounds). To produce a word, the child not only has to complete this process but now has to assign a known word (from the stored lexicon) to the combination of sounds. The word has to be in the lexicon of the brain otherwise the child may pronounce a nonsense-sounding word or may say the word but not recognise it or know what it means. This indirect route puts far greater pressure on the short-term memory of the brain. This is very difficult for dyslexic children.

In reality most children learn by both routes and an efficient reader automatically switches from one system to the other. If a word does not immediately register in the lexicon of the visual route the brain switches to phonemic analysis. Inefficient readers and children with dyslexia do not do this automatically and have to be taught to do it. They need to be taught different ways of decoding, not just one. We must not forget at this point what reading is actually about. The recommendation to use synthetic phonics and the requirement of 'fidelity to the programme' may be counterproductive to overall reading development for some children. Ofsted (2008) found that most schools *are working faithfully within the structure of their chosen programme and teaching phonemes and graphemes in the specified order.* This is a little worrying when the uniqueness of individualised programmes for dyslexic children is considered.

Reading is about meaning. Henderson (2008) notes that there is far less research surrounding the measurement of understanding of text.

As you can see from the above, reading is a collection of sub-skills and mental processes which occur together but also partially independently as outlined by Curran (2008) in his model of how the brain works.

The sub-skills can be outlined as follows.
- Visual analysis.
- Acquiring a lexicon – a store of known words and their patterns.
- Semantic knowledge from using their own language and from being read to.
- Grapheme-to-phoneme conversion (this encompasses the two skills of letter recognition and sound allocation).
- Blending of the sounds identified.
- Output of either a visually recognised word or a blended word.

Each of these methods of teaching reading – look and say or word recognition and phonics – ignores a crucial aspect of reading: meaning. When a child is engaged in the task of reading in the context of a book or a notice, there are far more clues available than in single-word reading. Wider linguistic clues such as vocabulary, grammar/syntax and semantics are brought to bear on the process as well as bibliographic details such as pictures and subheadings, etc.

The debate about phonics versus look and say will continue into generations to come, each claiming 'proof' that one system is better than another. Fox (2005) clearly states the case for meaningful language tuition rather than focused reading tuition when she outlines how young gifted readers learn to read by being read to, by being immersed in the language, and she makes the point that no parent sets out to teach their child phonics but rather engages in a meaningful language exchange and reads to their child for pleasure. She further makes the point that phonics can differ from one area to another and from one country to another according to the local accent and that in these cases phonics tuition becomes a rather meaningless exercise. In these circumstances it is certainly not foolproof.

She offers the following as proof that phonics is not essential to acquiring reading and meaning:

> *Aoccdrnig to rscheearch at an Elingsh Uinervtisy, it deosn't mttaer in what order the ltteers in a word are, the only iprmoetnt thing is that the frist and lsat ltteers are in the rghit pclae: the rset can be a total mses but you can still raed it wouthit a porbelm. This is bcuseae we don't raed ervey lteter but the word as a wlohe.*

However, there is now research evidence to suggest that teaching phonics helps the brains of dyslexic children (and adults) to develop and grow in areas where they are underdeveloped or to change the brain activity. Research by Richards et al. (2000) indicates that sustained tuition in phonics can minimise the difference between dyslexic brain activity and non-dyslexic brain activity. The same study found that dyslexic brains were working nearly five times harder than non-dyslexic brains to complete the same activity prior to the intensive tuition. Dyslexia-teacher (www.dyslexia-teacher.com) provides a good summary of this research. Eden et al. (2004) support and extend this research to include improvements in adults with developmental dyslexia; reporting improvements in phonological processing as well as single-word reading and a generalised development of the function of the left hemisphere of the brain. They report that areas of the brain which had previously been underactive were now provoked into activity following tuition. Perhaps phonics tuition would be worthwhile for this result if not for any reading benefits.

Reading Recovery

Reading Recovery is a programme which was introduced in Great Britain in a piecemeal fashion to start with but has gathered momentum and government funding in the past three years. 'Every child a reader' which has been funded from 2005 to 2008, has seen an increase in the number of Reading Recovery teachers being trained. Reading Recovery uses many of the features of good individualised dyslexia tuition. Each child receives an individualised programme designed around their specific needs after an assessment and this is on a one-to-one basis for 30 minutes every day. The programme is different for every child. The Institute for Education website states that *the starting point is the child's strengths and the teaching builds upon what the child is able, and is trying to do*. This is very similar to the philosophy put forward in this book and is in line with good dyslexia teaching but it is not consistent with a prescriptive order for teaching phonics as endorsed by Letters and Sounds (DfES, 2007), the government programme for teaching phonics. In Reading Recovery each child receives 30 hours of teaching over 12 weeks. It is aimed at the lowest-achieving third of each class without exception. There are no reading tests or reading lag criteria to meet. Unfortunately, because of teacher mobility the number of teachers has dropped dramatically. Also a number of schools have stopped using it because of financial constraints when the funding ends.

Overview

There are various methods to teach decoding of words.

With dyslexic children something goes amiss with the process.

There are various theories about the causes of dyslexia and why dyslexic children have difficulties with reading, spelling and mathematics.

Reading is about more than decoding.

Reading is about extracting meaning regardless of the means by which this is achieved. Even if a child has received tuition in either/all of the different methods of decoding texts, if they are unable to make any use of this then they cannot be said to be reading in any meaningful sense.

Dyslexic children expend more energy to achieve the same results and may be slower in reading and comprehending.

Mathematics

Similarly, mathematics is affected in the learning of tables when the information is acquired in the left-hand side of the brain but there are then difficulties with processing the information in the right-hand side of the brain coupled with working memory difficulties. Curran (2008) states: *Another specialised area in your left hemisphere is that dealing with mathematics. Whilst your right hemisphere is involved in processing mathematical data as well, most of the processing seems to occur in your left hemisphere especially as the sums get more difficult.*

What does this all mean in the classroom?

Consequences of dyslexia

Most often the consequences of dyslexia impact on the education of the child in a very overt way. The child will display slow learning, development which is different from most other children. Notwithstanding Pollock and Waller's (1997) understanding that all children learn in different ways, that not all children are rounded learners nor that all children are all round learners, and Gardner's (2008) work on multiple intelligences, it can still be noted that there are certain markers that single out 'at risk' children from others if the classroom teacher knows what to be alert to. It is no longer tenable to dismiss children who are experiencing difficulty as immature in their learning or to claim they will eventually catch up. Various court judgements as well as moral arguments have thankfully put an end to this rather lax attitude.

Motivation

Regardless of the techniques for decoding, motivation is everything. Without motivation to read and to continue to read, children will only learn patchily. Rosen (2008) the current children's laureate, criticises the literacy hour for killing off enjoyment. The same news article reports Jim Rose as indicating that boys particularly need topics to interest them, not hours spent analysing texts. Games and play provide that motivation.

The following correlations may be observed but for detailed symptoms and signs read Chapter 2 on screening. Table 1.1 is a generalised outline of main developmental aspects:

Table 1.1 Skill deficit linked to practical outcome

Skill	Leads to
Poor short-term auditory memory	Cannot hold information for long, leads to difficulty in mathematics, following instructions, spelling, remembering what has been heard and auditory attention.
Poor visual memory	Makes remembering shapes and patterns difficult, which means copying is hard, spelling and reading may be affected, remembering tables even if written in front of them.
Poor auditory sequencing	Difficulty in organising material in the correct order, leads to difficulty with spelling and oral tables, the alphabet, reading comprehension, following instructions.
Poor visual sequencing	Organising information is difficult, particularly spelling (especially irregular words), copying, reading comprehension.
Poor visuomotor co-ordination	Difficulties with writing, poor posture, PE affected balance, ball skills and batting.
Visuospatial	Perception of space and shape is affected and leads to poor page payout and handwriting with irregular size, slant, shape, etc. They can also be clumsy, knocking into items or people, may spill equipment such as paint, etc.
Comprehension	Understanding the spoken word can often be difficult and may lead to incorrect following of instructions, may not understand stories, etc. May take visual cues from others.
Auditory discrimination	Difficulty in hearing fine differences leads to incorrect reading and spelling, may mispronounce words. May have difficulty with onset and rime or analogy. Hearing tests may not pick this up. You have to be observant for this.
Phonological awareness	Perception of sounds may not be developed, may have difficulty in sequencing sounds in words, again pronouncing words incorrectly. May have difficulty with alliteration rhyme, identification of phonemes.
Poor speed in processing	Slow processing will lead to the child being slower in almost everything which involves incoming information and in output of information. They will be slower in reading, comprehending, writing and in articulating what they want to say even when it is correct in its final version.

Fine motor skills may be affected	Leads to
Unable to maintain grip	Spidery writing or overly heavy pressure on pens and pencils to point of breaking.
Poor concept of position in space	Poor layout of writing, inability to colour in or keep between lines,
Poor dexterity	Difficulty with personal care such as tying shoes, closing buttons, etc.
Visual perception may be affected	Leads to
Poor visual tracking and locating	Difficulty in keeping place, may skip lines or reread a line, confusion of similar letters.
Poor visual perception	Difficulty in distinguishing foreground from background, difficulty in distinguishing individual letters or words from the background.

Children with dyslexia not only lag behind in academic subjects but often their self-confidence is harmed. Social skills can also be affected with an overly exaggerated display of emotion. It is not uncommon for children to show signs of frustration, isolation or withdrawal (particularly with girls), depression, bullying behaviour. Playground staff need to be alert to the secondary or soft signs of learning disabilities otherwise the child may just get into trouble and become more disenchanted with school. They may also take on the role of the 'class clown' if they are clumsy. In extreme circumstances they may opt out of school; truanting or just becoming disengaged and unco-operative in school. At home parents may note bed-wetting and changes in mood and appetite. Ofsted (1999) noted that a *benefit of early intervention is that pupils are less likely to experience emotional problems as a result of failure.*

Co-morbid conditions

A full examination of the relationship between other conditions and dyslexia is beyond the scope of this book. Nor can this book outline the nature of other conditions but it would be remiss not to mention other conditions which very often manifest alongside dyslexia in children. How many of the symptoms displayed are due to dyslexia or to the other condition is a matter for a specialist to determine; however, you need to be aware that dyslexia often does not just occur on its own. Very often children who are dyslexic will also be dyspraxic or have attention deficit hyperactivity disorder (ADHD) (with or without the hyperactivity) and many children who are predominantly on the autistic spectrum will have some dyslexia.

This can lead to an interesting and frustrating mix of signs and symptoms. It is important for you to be aware of this overlap of conditions because a child may display only a limited number of the signs for dyslexia but may be predominantly ADHD and it would be easy to assign all of their difficulties to ADHD and ignore the dyslexia signs.

Working with parents and other family members

Parents are key partners when working with children with dyslexia. They are often ignored as worthy of mention when looking at the impact of dyslexia. However, the impact of dyslexia is not confined to the classroom: it affects social development and family relationships. Not only will you often find that there is a family history of dyslexia but the impact of dyslexia affects not only the child but parents and other siblings as well. There may well be a family history of dyslexia which not only gives the parents a first-hand experience of what the child is experiencing, but may also lead to feelings of guilt or inevitability about their child being dyslexic.

Often the parent will have noticed that their child is having difficulty and it may be that the parent has already brought their concerns to the school. If they have not and you are the first person to mention it to them, there may be an element of surprise, disbelief and denial. Alternatively there may be a feeling of relief to find out that there is a genuine reason why their child is having difficulties. A meeting about a child who is having difficulty should always be attended by the SENCo if possible. It should take an open-question style of information gathering. You may be dreading having to tell the parents that their child is having difficulty when in fact the parents have known this for a while and can even offer you a possible reason for it.

Parents are key in supporting the child at home and in the broader aspect of organisation. You will need to involve the parents as real partners throughout the process. Parents may need support themselves; they may blame themselves or think they have done something wrong. They may feel inadequate in supporting the child. You can provide a lot of support and contacts for parents feeling like this. You need to keep regular contact with the parents outside the review process.

Working with other professionals

When you teach a child with dyslexia you will automatically come into contact with a host of other professionals who are ready to give support and advice. The educational psychologist usually will be involved in writing an assessment report, although this can sometimes be undertaken by a suitably qualified assessment teacher. Your authority may employ advisory teachers to support English and language development; they are often less likely to be able to help than the special needs support staff although some English advisory staff will also be qualified in teaching dyslexic children.

Professional associations often have a staff that is able and willing to help. The British Dyslexia Association has a list of qualified teachers in the area that may be willing to come into school and offer advice. These staff will be trained in multisensory teaching.

If the child also has language difficulties you may come into contact with a speech therapist although these appear to be a dying breed in many authorities. A child with dyspraxia will be under the observation of a physiotherapist who may provide exercises for you to carry out in school. It is important that you work with these professionals. You can offer your opinion and very often they will ask for your input regarding how the child behaves and manages in school; this is why it is important for you to keep detailed notes as part of your monitoring system.

Other teachers in the school and teaching assistants will work with pupils with learning difficulties from time to time and will need to know the learning profile of the pupil and the further implications of being dyslexic. Ofsted (1999) noted that *not all the relevant teachers were sufficiently aware of these implications, or of the targets in the pupils' individual education plans*. It is your responsibility to brief these other professionals working with children on a day-to-day basis or even on the occasional basis.

A SUMMARY OF **KEY POINTS**

> **There are varied hypotheses regarding the cause and nature of dyslexia.**

> **All hypotheses must be responded to in the context of educational achievement or lack of it.**

> **Dyslexia is the most prevalent learning difficulty in schools today.**

> **You need to involve the parents as soon as you suspect their child may be 'at risk'.**

> **Dyslexia can lead to other challenges for the teacher such as low self-esteem and poor behaviour.**

MOVING *ON* > > > > > > MOVING *ON* > > > > > > MOVING *ON*

Attend any courses provided by your local authority or the professional associations such as the BDA, or DyslexiaAction.

Talk to dyslexic people, adults and children about what it is like to be dyslexic; in this way you will gain a greater understanding of the condition.

REFERENCES REFERENCES **REFERENCES** REFERENCES **REFERENCES** REFERENCES

BBC (2005) Scientists discover dyslexia gene www.news.bbc.co.uk/1/hi/health/4384414.stm (accessed 22/8/08)

BPS British Psychological Society (1999) at www.countmein.org.uk/explanations/definitions (accessed 20/12/08)

Chia, N (1996) The tri continua model of dyslexic syndrome. *Education Today*, 46 (3): 33–40

Curran, A (2008) *The little book of big stuff about the brain*. Camarthen: Crown House Publishing

Denckia, M and Rudel, R (1976) Rapid 'automatized' naming (RAN) Dyslexia differentiated from other learning disabilities. *Neuropyschologia* 14: 471–9

DfES (2001) *Special Educational Needs Code of Practice*. DfES2001581/2001 London: Department for Education and Skills

DfES (2007) *Letters and sounds*. London: Department for Education and Skills

Eden, G, Jones, K, Cappell, K, Gareau, L, Wood, F, Zeffiro, T, Dietz, N, Agnew, J and Flowers, D (2004) Neural changes following remediation in adult developmental dyslexia. *Neuron*, 44: 411–22

Equalities and Human Rights Commission www.equalityhumanrights.com/en/yourrights/equalityand discrimination/Disability/Pages/Introduction.aspx (accessed 25/8/08)

Fox, M (2005) *Reading magic*. Sydney: Pan Macmillan

Gardner, H (2008) Howard Gardner, multiple intelligences and education, www.infed.org/thinkers/gardner.htm

Gillhooly, D (2008) The ECJ confirms that the Disability Discrimination Act needs to change. *TES* 24/7/2008

Henderson, L (2008) Understanding readings. *The Psychologist* 3/6/2008

Henry, J (2002a) Alarm at talk of dyslexia miracle. *TES* 8/2/2002

Henry, J (2002b) Row over claims of dyslexia cure. *TES* 8/2/2002

House of Lords Dyslexia Debate 7 December 2005 accessible at BDA: www.bdadyslexia.org.uk/downloads/Lords.pdf accessed (15/9/08)

Irlen, H (1991) *Scotopic sensitivity syndrome – screening manual.* Long Beach, CA: Perceptual Development Corporation

Kelly, B (1998) Dyslexia/reading difficulty: reassessing the evidence for a developmental model. *Education Today*, 40 (1): 3–17

Livingstone, M, Rosen, G, Drisaine, F and Galaburda, A (1991) Physiological and anatomical evidence for a magnocellular defect in developmental dyslexia. *Proceedings of the National Academy of Science of the United States of America*, 88: 7943–7

Lowenstein, L (1996) Dyslexia: a review of Literature. *Education Today* 46 (3): 25–32

Miles, (1996) A hundred years of dyslexia in Britain, in *The Dyslexia Handbook 1996* (ed. by Julia Crisfield). Bracknell: The British Dyslexia Association

Nicolson, R and Fawcett, A (1990) Automaticity: a new framework for dyslexic research? *Cognition* 35(2) 159–82

Ofsted (1999) *Pupils with specific learning difficulties in mainstream schools.* London: HMSO

Ofsted (2004) *Special educational needs and disability: towards inclusive schools.* London: Ofsted

Ofsted (2008) *Responding to the Rose Review: schools' approaches to the systematic teaching of phonics,* ref. no. 080038. London: Ofsted

Ott, P (1997) *How to detect and manage dyslexia.* Oxford: Heinemann

Perfetti, CA (1985) *Reading ability.* Oxford: Oxford University Press

Pollock, J and Waller, E (1997) *Day-to-day dyslexia in the classroom.* Abingdon: Routledge Falmer

Ramus, F (2001) Dyslexia – talk of two theories. *Nature* 412(6845), 393–5

Richards, T, Corina, D, Serafini, S, Steury, K, Echelard, D, Dager, S, Marro, K, Abbott, R, Maravilla, K and Berninger, V (2000) Effects of a phonologically-driven treatment for dyslexia on lactate levels measured by proton MR spectroscope imaging. *American Journal of Neuroradiology*, 21: 916–22

Reid, G (2004) *Dyslexia – a practitioner's handbook.* (3rd edn) Chichester: Wiley

Rosen, M (2008) How do we fire children's enthusiasm to read? *Guardian.co.uk Mortarboard Blog,* www.guardian.co.uk/education/mortarboard/2008/sep/02/schools.primaryschools (accessed 2/9/08)

Schumacher, J, Hoffmann, P, Schmal, C, Schulte-Korne, G and Nothen, M (2007) Genetics of dyslexia: the evolving landscape. *Journal of Medical Genetics*, 44: 289–97

Smythe, I (2008) Dislexia, dyslecsia, diszlexia, dyslexi – but is it dyslexia? *Dyslexia Contact*, 27: 3 September 2008

Stein, J and Walsh, V (1997) To see but not to read: the magnocellular theory of dyslexia. Trends in *Neurosciences Journal* 1997; 20: 147–52

Taipale, M, Kaminen, N, Nopola-Hemmi, J, Haltia, T, Myllyluoma, B, Lyytinen, H, Muller, K, Kaaranen, M, Lindsberg, P, Hannula-Jouppi, K and Kere, J (2003) A candidate gene for developmental dyslexia encodes a nuclear tetratricopeptide repeat domain protein dynamically regulated in brain. *Proceedings of National Academy of Sciences of United States of America* 30 September 2003, 100(20): 11553–8

US National Institute of Child Health and Human Development (2002) www.nih.gov/science/ (accessed Dec 2008)

Yap, R and Vanderleij, A (1993) Word processing in dyslexics – an automatic decoding deficit. *Reading and Writing*, 5(3): 261–79

FURTHER READING FURTHER READING **FURTHER READING** FURTHER READING

Dyslexic children use nearly five times the brain area. www.dyslexia-teacher.com/t101.html

Report on House of Lords Dyslexia Debate 7 December 2005, www.bdadyslexia.org.uk/downloads/Lords.pdf

2
Identifying dyslexia – some practical strategies

Chapter objectives

By the end of this chapter you should be aware of:

- **the main signs and symptoms of dyslexia;**
- **the difficulties many dyslexic children encounter in learning;**
- **a variety of games and activities which will inform your observations of children you consider 'at risk';**
- **how to refer a child to an educational psychologist or assessment teacher.**

This chapter addresses the following Professional Standards for QTS:

Q5, Q11, Q12, Q13, Q26(b), Q27, Q28, Q29.

Introduction

There have been a number of news articles which recount how a teacher has not identified a child's dyslexia and therefore the appropriate provision has not been put in place. Screening, rather than diagnosis, can and should be carried out by all teachers. Screening and assessment should inform any teaching which takes place. The profile of strengths and weaknesses which results from screening and assessment is of prime importance in addressing the individual needs of the child. Even if you think after screening that the child is not 'at risk', you will have gathered vital information which will still inform your understanding of that child.

Theoretical background

Screening is a crucial aspect of satisfying the SEN Code of Practice (DfES, 2001) and there are many references to assessment and screening in various government documents. The Code of Practice (DfES, 2001) states: *The importance of early identification, assessment and provision for any child who may have special educational needs cannot be overemphasised* (5:11). More recently, Letters and Sounds (DfES, 2007) promotes ongoing formative and diagnostic assessment as an integral part of learning and teaching. As mentioned in the last chapter, some schools are creating ability groups across different ages and classes. While early identification is endorsed, such 'setting' at so young an age cannot be a positive development for many children. This practice is more in keeping with Key Stage 3 provision.

As a class teacher you will be constantly assessing the children in your class. Some may exceed your expectations, many will fall within the normal range; however, some will cause you concern because they are not progressing. It is these children you need to focus on for extra information about why they are not progressing.

Once you realise how varied and extensive dyslexia is, you will start to wonder how you can identify children who may be at risk, you will worry about labelling a child wrongly as dyslexic or whether you are causing concern where there is no need. These are natural worries. No teacher wants to alarm parents unnecessarily; however you also have a duty, under the SEN Code of Practice (DfES, 2001), to the child to identify any barriers to their learning. There are numerous packs available to plot profiles of children and many of the activities here are drawn from such packs. The folders *The National Literacy Strategy Supporting Pupils Working Significantly Below Age-Related Expectations* (DfEE, 2000) and *Early Literacy Support* (DfEE, 2001) provide many activities which can focus observation. There is a section on screening during the literacy hour and focused activities for screening for word-level understanding, reading, writing and speaking and listening. There are many resources such as common word grids which will prove useful for many practitioners. These activities are rather general and quite formal; the activities suggested in this chapter are taken from more specific packs related to dyslexia and are more specific to the sub-skills which are affected in dyslexia.

Activities such as the following are not new and were often commonplace in the Reception class of the 1970s. They slowly lost prominence because they often seemed purposeless. This is the danger of practice with no theoretical underpinning – you do not know why you are doing something and find it hard to defend when challenged. The National Curriculum of 1988 also brought about a change in practice so that play activities were often seen as time-wasting and not real education. These activities rightly have a place not only in the teaching of young children but are instrumental in screening and assessment of young children. The child who has difficulty completing a jigsaw puzzle is not just displaying their difficulty with this one game but is also likely to be displaying an issue which is crucial to reading – the ability to see a part of a whole picture.

While screening can be undertaken at classroom level it is crucial that, once you identify a child who is not progressing along with their peers or displays difficulty in one specific area, you refer them on to an appropriate person who can thoroughly assess and diagnose any real learning difficulties such as dyslexia, dyspraxia or ADHD. This level of assessment is beyond the qualifications of most classroom teachers unless of course they hold an appropriate qualification. However, this identification is crucial, with early assessment being paramount as the Code of Practice endorses: *The earlier action is taken, the more responsive the child is likely to be, and the more readily can intervention be made without undue disruption to the organisation of the school* (DfES, 2001, 5:11).

Screening should be undertaken sensitively and consistently and set over a time period: *assessment should not be regarded as a single event but rather as a continuing process* (DfES, 2001). This process starts with the class teacher or sometimes with the classroom teaching assistant.

It may be necessary to take a child out of the classroom to undertake some screening tasks in a quiet room. In this instance it would be good practice to have taken the child to a quiet room for other activities first so that they do not think that they are in trouble, or taking a test. This type of anxiety can produce false results in screening.

Screening should also be self-checked: you may want to check the same aspect several times over before you consider that the child really is performing consistently and is at risk.

It is crucial that you are using correct terminology and enunciating phonemes accurately when assessing children. If these are not carried out carefully you may be disadvantaging a child. This is particularly relevant since Ofsted (2008) found that *occasionally there is a lack of accuracy in enunciating phonemes, some uncertainty in the use of terminology and some insecurity about assessment* (p4). It is important that your own knowledge facilitates detailed screening and ongoing assessment against normal classroom resources rather than hampers it. It is equally important that you are confident to ascertain prior learning and to start from where the child is, since Rose (2008) in the Interim Review of the Curriculum found that *many Year 1 teachers began to introduce the subjects of the National Curriculum at the start of the autumn term, irrespective of the pupils' prior attainment* (p56). This is quite disconcerting since individualised learning is endorsed in the Interim Report; however, Rose recommends that further moderation is undertaken to increase teachers' understanding of the Early Years Foundation Stage goals and their confidence in Reception teachers' assessments. Rose further outlines: *Securing progress which builds on children's prior learning is a central curricular objective. Because progress is goal related, the goals of learning must be explicit in order to guide planning and teaching, whether cross-curricular or focussed on discrete subject content* (p5). This would seem to confirm the use of focused assessments linked to staged progression in the teaching of early reading, namely synthetic phonics. Nowhere in the document does Rose mention either dyslexia or learning difficulties. This does seem to be anomalous with his aspirations of individualised learning in Key Stage 1. It also places a considerable responsibility on teachers in the near future in terms of knowledge, confidence and competence in addressing the needs of all children.

You need to consider other factors, apart from your own ability, which might influence the outcome of an assessment or screening activity.

- Previous teaching – has the child been taught those aspects you are screening for?
- Attendance – has the child been in school to benefit from tuition?
- Other illnesses – has the child had other illnesses which could impact on learning?
- Hearing/sight history/testing – has the child had a recent sensory test? Are you in an area where intermittent hearing loss is common through 'glue ear'?
- Background – has the child been exposed to 'normal' language development activities such as hearing stories read, nursery rhymes, play-writing, etc.?

REFLECTIVE TASK

Consider what evidence is already available about a particular child in your class. What extra evidence might you want to collect and how would you go about it?

Signs of dyslexia in early childhood

- Inability to complete tasks other children learn such as buttoning coat, using knife and fork.
- Slow in learning motor skills such as climbing stairs, riding a bike.
- Searching for words and coming up with a near miss such as 'lamppost' for 'lamp shade'.
- Often they may have other speech problems such as a lisp.
- Slow in learning phoneme–grapheme correspondence.
- Slow in learning to write own name and other common words.
- Unable to produce rhyming words in games, etc.

Signs at Key Stage 1

Many of the above are still prevalent with children in the 4–7 year age group. In addition they may exhibit the following.

- Difficulty with writing – letter formation, construction of sentences, layout on the page, etc.
- Further difficulties with reading – not being able to learn sight words and not being able to build up words phonetically, not being able to cut words into syllables or onset and rime.
- Short attention span and difficulty with concentration.
- Some aspects of disruptive behaviour may be starting to emerge at this point too, particularly at the end of Key Stage 1.
- Avoidance strategies include the following:
  - requesting to go to the toilet frequently;
  - changing the subject;
  - losing items in order not to complete the task;
  - returning to the back of the queue for help and never reaching the front of the queue.
- Avoidance strategies at the top of Key Stage 2 are more prevalent in boys than girls and tend to be more disruptive, with boys calling out, joking inappropriately, refusing to co-operate, causing disturbances with children around them. Girls tend to be more withdrawn and just wander around the room or do not complete their work. They often feign illness as a reason for not completing work.

Signs at Key Stage 2

- Aspects such as inability when doing up buttons may still be evident or inability to tie shoelaces but have often been overcome by strategies such as wearing self fastening shoes, wearing jumpers or jackets that have zips rather than buttons.
- Spelling becomes increasingly random and idiosyncratic at Key Stage 2.
- Incomplete writing or writing of poor quality or length is evident.
- Slow and laboured writing.
- Reluctance to read.
- Tiredness after reading.
- Cannot make sense of what has been read.
- Child may be well behind peers in learning times tables and number bonds.
- Confusion of left and right – difficulty with following directions.
- Lack of organisation – forgets books, tasks, loses items easily.
- Behaviour may be a real problem by Key Stage 2, particularly in boys.
- Boys may become more aggressive, more foolhardy and attempt to gain attention through being a 'class clown'.
- Or they may become belligerent when faced with work they perceive as too hard and may become troublesome and disruptive in the class.
- Girls tend to become more withdrawn and quiet, often evading work by just keeping a low profile in the class. They may feign sickness in order to gain sympathy and an attitude of tolerance. This can turn into manipulation.

A further list of detailed descriptors can be found in Hornsby (1995).

Hyperlexia

Hyperlexia often goes unnoticed or is little understood. This aspect of dyslexia is related to constructing meaning and affects the understanding of reading and the construction of the written word. These children often have very good memory function and can learn spellings easily, unlike most other dyslexic children.

Because of this good memory they can usually pass any spelling test and read word-perfectly so they often are not picked up in normal classroom tests. However, they have extreme difficulty in answering inferential questions related to what they have read and in constructing a sensible piece of written work. Their writing is often marked by the absence of function words to create a full sentence, their writing being made up of the important content words only.

Dyslexia as a syndrome

To suspect that a child might be dyslexic it is not sufficient for them to display just one of the above criteria. They need to display a few of them, consistently. The behaviour should also be inconsistent with their age, development or other factors such as teaching. What is meant here is that it is normal for most four-year-olds to confuse left and right but most children are taught or grow out of this by the time they are eight years old. Most children have difficulty with spellings at some point but most eight-year-olds have learnt strategies in order to learn the majority of spellings given to them. Many children if not motivated will produce inade-quate writing but are often motivated to write at length on subjects that interest them. When looking at a child, you need to put all the factors together: does this child consistently produce inadequate writing? Do they always have difficulty with learning spellings? Do they have other signs such as lack of co-ordination? It is only when you can say they satisfy the dyslexic profile that you would consider referring them on, although it would be wise to discuss this with your SENCo as the final decision rests with them.

REFLECTIVE TASK

Consider the children in your class. How many of them exhibit more than one of the above criteria? How many exhibit most of them? What is being done to support these children?

Screening children

Screening activities need to be age appropriate; however, most can be adapted to suit the age of child.

Screening for auditory memory difficulties

- Robotic spelling – prepare a list of simple words which you will split up phoneme by phoneme; words such as cat, boat, blast, are good. Don't make the words too long, for example – 'interspersed'. Turn the child around so they are facing the other way and say the phonemes; the child has to produce the correct word from the phonemes. Record the word they actually say.
- Non-word blending – use a list of non-words such as that provided in Johnston and Watson (2007) to ascertain whether the child can blend sounds making non-words. This is harder than real-word blending above.
- Same or different – select pairs of words which sound nearly the same such as boat and coat, hat and mat, and select some that are the same such as dog and dog. While the child is facing away from you say the pairs of words and ask the child to say if they are the same or different. Record each answer.
- Digit memory. Have ready a sequence of numbers starting with three-digit sequences and building to six

digits. Say the digits to the child and ask them to repeat the sequence to you. Record their answers. Repeat this but this time the child has to say the digits in reverse order. For example, if you say '391' the child has to say '193'. Record their answers exactly.

- Play games such as 'I went to the market and bought'.
- Make up your own silly sentences such as 'I fought 24 pink elephants when along came 45 ostriches to help them'. Get the child to repeat back to you.
- Play 'Simon says' and watch for the children who cannot retain the instruction or remember that they only respond when 'Simon says'.
- Other activities are provided in the back of Johnston and Watson (2007), including segmenting words and blending together again, deletion of initial and final phonemes from words.

Screening for visual memory difficulties

- Prepare a picture card with a sequence of shapes/beads on it. To start use no more than four and build up from there. Use either 2D maths shapes such as triangles, squares, diamonds, etc. or 3D beads of different shapes and colours. Show the child the card with the pattern on it for around 15 seconds for them to store this pattern in their brain. Now ask them to replicate the pattern with the resources in front of them. You could of course use a second string of beads or 2D shapes but you would need to cover these once viewed.
- Prepare a set of pictures with mirror images. Have duplicates ready for the child to lay out. Show them a pattern of three to start with, give them around 15 seconds to memorise the pattern and then cover it and ask them to replicate the pattern from a selection of six which includes the correct pictures. Record exactly their responses.
- Have pairs of cards bearing visual images ready. Start with one visual image on each card, building up to four visual images on each card. The images can be either pictures or symbols such as squares, etc. Show the child the first pair. Allow only a minimal amount of time for them to look at it; 5 seconds is as long as you should allow. Now take the cards away and ask the child: were the cards the same of different? Record their answers.
- Observe how a child tackles a jigsaw puzzle. Being able to make sense of a whole picture from bits of it is a crucial skill in reading and spelling.
- Ask a child to replicate a letter in the sand or using modelling clay.
- Play letter bingo allowing them only a few seconds to look at the prompt letter.
- Play pairs where the child has to look at a pair of words (either identical or a minimal pair). They may only look for a second or two and have to say whether the words were the same or different.

Other screening activities (select according to age)

Check the child knows the phonemes and names of the letters of the alphabet, check they can arrange the alphabet in the correct order. A score sheet is available at the back of Johnston and Watson (2007) or you can make your own.

You will also observe the child daily and make field notes of errors and strengths. Typical errors of spelling and maths are outlined by Pollock and Waller (2001).

Air writing

Turn the child around and draw a letter on their back with your finger. Say how you write the letter as you do it. For example, for the letter b you might say 'this letter starts at the top comes down to the line, goes up again and goes over a bump then joins the down stroke again'. The child has to guess the letter you have drawn on their back. To take it a stage further you could ask the child to provide a word starting with that phoneme.

Check the child has good concepts of print, i.e. that they know the correct orientation of a book, that they know the print should be read left to right and that print flows down the page. They should also be able to demarcate a letter, a word, a sentence. To test for this use two pieces of card and ask the child to move the card until all that can be seen in the gap between the two pieces of card is the letter or word, etc.

It is important to record the strengths as well as weaknesses of children so that you have a profile of that child (Pollock and Waller, 2001). Celebrating the strengths of pupils will boost their self-confidence, and this is an aspect which requires attention with dyslexic pupils. Inclusion of the child's perspective on their difficulties is also important and easily over-looked. It may be that the child thinks they have difficulties in areas that you have not considered; this is especially true of older children. By including children you have an opportunity to affirm their strengths as well as reveal perceived inadequacies. This is espe-cially crucial for children who may, if it were not for their literacy difficulties, be gifted or very able (Montgomery, 2000).

While you are observing generally you will notice signs that a child is developing either more slowly or differently than other children. Note down when they search for words or produce the wrong word for the sentence. Observe when they seem not to be able to locate personal items such as their drawer or coat hanger if these are marked by symbols, as they often are in Reception year. Watch them when they are getting dressed after PE. Watch them in the yard: are they co-ordinated like other children or do they lack gross/fine motor co-ordina-tion? Are they being prevented from participating in games such as skipping because of this?

Wall (2003) provides advice on further activities for observation and assessment.

Referring on

Before an educational psychologist assesses a child you will have had to compile a folder of information and worked with your SENCo to produce evidence to support your concern that the child is potentially dyslexic. You will need to have utilised programmes to support the child and followed an Individual Education Plan (IEP). These may either be your own programmes or a published programme such as THRASS to assist with different aspects of dyslexia. Examples of IEPs can be found in both the Code of Practice (DfES, 2001) and the folder: *Primary National Strategy Leading on Inclusion* (DfES, 2005).

You should also at an early stage have involved the parents and shared your observations with them. Note I say observations rather than concerns. It is important to keep parents informed but not to worry them unnecessarily. You will also probably wish to gain the parents' perceptions and any information they can provide you with about the child's history or about familial literacy difficulties. Porter (2002) provides an excellent rationale for working with parents. If you have kept careful notes of both the strengths and the difficulties the child is experiencing and the teaching programmes you have used, those aspects which have been successful and those that have not, your referral will be easier to process. Referring on can be undertaken independently by the parents or by the local authority. It depends which local authority (LA) you work in how quickly this happens and the criteria used. Some LAs will not take referrals until a child is two years behind chronological age in reading tests, as noted above. This obviously pushes the age of referral up since most dyslexic children would not be referred on until they are at least seven years old. Some authorities use COPS, which is a computer program for screening 'at risk' children and refers any child who scores below the expected. This program includes activities such as those outlined above but notes not only recorded correct/incorrect answers but also computes the response time and compares it to a given norm.

It is important that you do not attempt to diagnose a child. This is the responsibility of a skilled and fully trained person with the appropriate qualifications. This person will use standardised tests as well as experienced observations to ascertain whether a child is dyslexic or not. Your role is to provide the background information and the observational data you have collected.

A SUMMARY OF **KEY POINTS**

> Observe and carry out specific focused screening activities on children you are concerned about or who seem not to be making progress.

> Make notes on all aspects of reading and sub-skills, do not just rely on a reading test or progression sheets obtained from a phonics programme.

> Keep careful notes of what you have done and the results.

> Liaise with parents.

> Liaise with your SENCo.

MOVING *ON* > > > > > > MOVING *ON* > > > > > > MOVING *ON*

Obtain a screening pack such as the Bangor screening kit or the Aston screening kit. Select a child you feel is 'at risk'. Note your own observations first then use one of these packages to confirm or refine your information. Discuss the outcomes with your SENCo or an advisory teacher from the LA.

REFERENCES REFERENCES **REFERENCES** REFERENCES **REFERENCES** REFERENCES

DfEE (2000) *The National Literacy Strategy Supporting Pupils Working Significantly Below Age-Related Expectations. Prolog ref. SPWBE.* London: Department for Education and Employment

DfEE (2001) *The National Literacy Strategy Early Literacy Support.* London: Department for Education and Employment

DfES (2001) *Special Educational Needs Code Of Practice ref DfES 2001581/2001).* London: Department for Education and Skills

DfES (2005) *Primary National Strategy Leading on Inclusion ref DfES 1183-2005G.* London: Department for Education and Skills

DfES (2007) *Letters and sounds.* London: Department for Education and Skills

Hornsby, B (1995) *Overcoming dyslexia. A straightforward guide for families and teachers.* London: Vermillion

Johnston, R and Watson, J (2007) *Teaching synthetic phonics.* Exeter: Learning Matters

Montgomery, D (ed.) (2000) *Able underachievers.* London: Whurr Publishers

Ofsted (2008) *Responding to the Rose Review: schools' approaches to the systematic teaching of phonics.* London: Ofsted

Pollock, J and Waller, E. (2001) *Day-to-day dyslexia in the classroom.* Abingdon: Routledge Falmer

Porter, L (2002) *Educating young children with special needs.* London: Paul Chapman Publishing

Rose, J (2008) *The independent review of the primary curriculum: interim report.* London: HMSO

Wall, K (2003) *Special needs and early years. A practitioner's guide.* London: Sage

3
Working with teaching assistants

Chapter objectives

By the end of this chapter you should be aware of:

- **the different roles undertaken by paraprofessionals, such as teaching assistants, in schools;**
- **the advantages and disadvantages of working with other adults;**
- **a selection of activities suitable for different teaching assistants.**

This chapter addresses the following Professional Standards for QTS:

Q20, Q24, Q30, Q32, Q33.

Introduction

The use of teaching assistants, especially high-level teaching assistants (HLTA), has become an area for professional development with both newly qualified and experienced teachers. Teachers, whose main aim has been to educate children, are now being required to manage other adults in the classroom. When this is done well it is to the benefit of all concerned, as evidenced by DfES (2000) and Wilson et al. (2003). This chapter will provide an overview of how to use your teaching assistant to support children with learning difficulties, especially dyslexia. Further guidance is provided in Hall (2004) and Hall (2005) in relation to using your teaching assistant and different learning difficulties.

Theoretical background

Teaching assistants form the mainstay for supporting children with special needs. By teaching assistant I mean the person who is not the teacher; this might include unqualified teaching assistants, high-level teaching assistants who have taken a general course, teaching assistants who have taken specific courses to support particular needs, learning mentors, classroom assistants, learning support assistants (LSA) or (learning) support workers. Regardless of the title I mean the person who is not the classroom teacher.

You will have gathered already that the teaching assistant can not only go by many names but that their level of training and involvement can vary not only from school to school but within a school.

Most schools now use some form of support in most classes.

Roles of the teaching assistant

The way in which teaching assistants are used varies according to what role or function you want them to have. These include the following.

- Working with individual children on academic work, either inside or outside the main classroom.
- Working with small groups of children on academic work, either inside or outside the main classroom.

- Supporting individual children with personal or emotional needs.
- Creating resources and adapting teaching materials for children but not having any direct input into teaching activities.
- Assisting the teacher with record-keeping and administrative duties.
- Other classroom duties such as wall displays and mending books.
- Covering for planning, preparation and assessment (PPA) time with the whole class, following the teacher's planning, while the teacher is absent from the room.
- Monitoring the rest of the class while the teacher teaches a focus group.

There is considerable evidence that the planned use of support assistants improves the literacy skills (as well as other skills) of those pupils they are engaged with. Some of the first findings came out of the National Evaluation Project reported by Wilson et al. (2003) as cited by Hall (2005), which reported positively on the benefits of working with teaching assistants. Savage and Carless (2005) also found that there was in fact a significant impact on attainment when working supporting children with poor literacy skills, and posed several questions for schools, LAs and trainers. They suggest that training LSAs to take a more active role could improve the literacy skills of 'at risk' pupils.' They pose the questions:

- *What are the advantages of LSAs' main deployment being with 'at risk' pupils?*
- *Does this approach raise any questions about the role of teachers and LSAs, or the way their deployment is perceived by pupils?*

This is in accord with the philosophy of Hall (2005), who suggests that continuing professional development should be provided for teaching assistants, and with Ofsted (2005), which states that *the work of classroom teaching assistants is carefully planned to ensure that identified pupils are provided with effective support*. HLTAs with qualifications and working to a set of professional standards are becoming more common and are a real resource for teachers and student teachers alike. In order to achieve Qualified Teacher Status you will need to demonstrate that you can manage teaching assistants.

Evidence from Wilson et al. (2007) also indicates that *Sixty per cent of HLTA respondents reported that they had a specialist role, most commonly in special education needs (SEN)*.

The first thing you need to do then when working with a teaching assistant is to find out what their job description is (if they have one) and what they expect to do and what they feel they can offer, what skills they have, etc. Many teaching assistants feel they are not valued and not taken into consideration as part of the teaching team but just treated as an extra pair of hands when in fact they could offer far more. While there are some teaching assistants who are unqualified and need support in this area, it is a mistake to assume all of your teaching assistants are less qualified or knowledgeable than you, although this may be so in some cases. Many teaching assistants have now undertaken training at different levels. There are some teaching assistants who have at least a first degree and have chosen to be a teaching assistant for a variety of reasons. Some reasons given are that this is a second or third career; having made their way in their first career, they now want just a job which is regular and draws on their skills and has some independence about it; some are returning to work after family breaks and find it difficult to return to previous careers. I have encountered teaching assistants who have previously been lawyers and want to be away from the cut and thrust of that environment and some who have been bankers and found it difficult to return to banking having taken a career break. Some do not now need the high earnings they trained for and are doing it for altruistic reasons, some are doing it for personal reasons because close contact with a family member with a learning difficulty has drawn their attention to the need for and reward in supporting children with learning difficulties. Ofsted (1999) noted the use of a former advisory teacher who was used to provide extra support to pupils with specific learning difficulties. The *Times Educational Supplement* of 1 March 2008 posed the following question: *Are you, or do you work with, graduates who are choosing to work as TAs in order to work in a stimulating and fulfilling (!) environment that fits in with family commitments?* Within two days over 30 posted responses were received, many citing not just TAs with degrees but some ex-teachers who no longer wish to take on the responsibilities that recent changes have brought to teaching but who still wish to work with children.

Each teaching assistant will have their own reasons for pursuing this line of work. Next get to know your teaching assistant personally. Find out what their personal beliefs and skills are. It would be disastrous to allocate support to your dyslexic children from the assistant who thinks all dyslexic children are shirkers or just lacking in intelligence. It would be equally disastrous to give them support from someone who may understand dyslexia but does not have the creativity to explain concepts in a meaningful way or who cannot adapt games and activities or shows exasperation that after ten different ways of showing a pupil how to work out a maths calculation they still cannot do it. This will take some sensitivity on your part and careful handling. This is something most teachers are not trained to do, to manage other staff and deploy work.

You will need to look at the suitability of your teaching assistant for what you want out of them and how you want them to support children with special needs, particularly dyslexia. You will also need to make the decision of how you group your children. You may have only one teaching assistant and it is often easier for all the children with special needs to be sitting on one table with the teaching assistant. However, pedagogically, this is not justifiable. You may have a child who has dyslexia but is highly intelligent and should be given adapted work at their own level rather than being placed on a table with children with real conceptual difficulties. There is also the danger that the teaching assistant may not see that this child needs support in comparison with other children who are struggling even more.

There are some classroom assistants who rather than working directly with children would prefer, and are better suited, to work supporting the teacher generally or undertaking supervised activities with the rest of the class. Hall (2005) outlines the skills suitable for each type of assistant. If you have a classroom assistant who is better at preparing material or generally supervising the class, this releases you to work with specific children. Whichever you choose, you will need to negotiate and discuss this with the teaching assistant. A good team does not just happen: it is like a good marriage, it takes working at. If you want your teaching assistant to work specifically with dyslexic children they need some training in this so you also need to make your outcomes explicit to them and include them in the planning. You need humility to listen to them if they suggest that what you propose is not feasible with dyslexic children and they may well suggest a different approach or task altogether. Ofsted (1999) noted the good practice of providing the teaching assistant and pupils with a copy of the lesson plan and targets so that not only could the teaching assistant adapt the activity but the pupils could then use it in the next lesson as a recap activity.

REFLECTIVE TASK

Make a list of the activities the TAs in your school undertake. Create a job description for them. Compare this with their actual job description (if they have one). Discuss with them how satisfied they are with what they do and if they feel they could be used to greater advantage. Do they seek training?

Required knowledge and understanding

Your teaching assistant supporting a dyslexic child will need the following knowledge and understanding.

- A basic knowledge of the normal development of language learning and mathematics.
- An understanding of how and why this is often delayed or disrupted in children with dyslexia.
- An understanding of the different subgroups of dyslexic children and how different strategies are needed for the extremes.
- An understanding of task analysis or 'tracking back' so that they can examine where the difficulty lies.
- An ability to think laterally and present information in different ways and be able to use concrete examples to which the children can relate.
- An ability to spot misconceptions and put these right.
- An appreciation of when to intervene and when to allow the child more time so that they discover the answer for themselves.
- An understanding of the emotional effects of dyslexia.
- An appreciation of the secondary effects of dyslexia and how to deal with them.

It is particularly important for the TA to know when to intervene, when to offer help and when to encourage children to try for themselves. Ofsted (2004) noted that often SEN children expect their schoolwork to be completed for them. They may come to learn dependence on the TA (Burden, 2005). However, there are also children who see asking

Personal attributes

- Ability to observe confidentiality.
- A calm and confident manner.
- A willingness to listen to children and to view learning from their point of view.
- Patience.
- Empathy with children to share and experience the joys and frustrations of being a child.
- The ability to articulate ideas in a way accessible to children.
- Creativity – to generate new ideas or ways of accomplishing a task.
- Practicality – the ability to devise practical examples and illustrations.
- Humour.
- Willingness to learn and to continue learning.
- Reliability. Nothing disrupts more than when you have planned a supported activity for the TA not to turn up and the child left needing assistance.

for help as a sign of failure and disgrace. It is equally important to develop an ethos of asking for help when needed right across the whole class. Ryan et al. (2001) noted that some SEN children develop help avoidance and do not ask for help even when they really need it.

Relationships with your teaching assistant

A good relationship is not a given. You may be lucky and get on well with your teaching assistant who may be older and/or more experienced than you. If, however, you do not get on like the proverbial 'house on fire', you have to hide your differences for the sake of the children. They should not be aware of tensions between you and your teaching assistant. There are some difficult situations that might need resolving. You need to be clear who is 'in charge' at any given time. If you are using your teaching assistant to work with a group, it would be insensitive if you interfere with the management of that group even if you can see that the TA is not handling the situation particularly well. If you do need to intervene you need to do so in a way that preserves the dignity of your teaching assistant. You could perhaps ask a problematic child to undertake a task which removes them from the group. You could then have a word with the child after the lesson and chat with the teaching assistant on what the difficulties were.

Similarly, if your teaching assistant is monitoring the rest of the class while you work with a group it is easy for them to assume you are still in overall charge and for you to assume they are going to deal with the management of the class so you don't need to be diverted from your specific input. Children will often pick up on this lack of certainty and exploit the situation to their advantage; behaviour can deteriorate rapidly.

Try to spend some time in the week observing and learning from your TA. Apart from the likelihood that they have known this group of children for longer than you have, they may well know strategies that you are not familiar with. They will also be pleased and flattered that you feel you can learn from them. There are many successful, experienced teachers who are recycling the combined skills of a number of TAs they have worked with over the years.

REFLECTIVE TASK

In a Reception classroom a newly qualified teacher/student is working in the class long term. There is an older and very experienced teaching assistant. The teaching assistant is accustomed to activities being done in a particular way. The teacher wishes to use different methods to help all of the children but particularly those children who are not responding to general teaching. She tries to introduce set routines such as having the large slide only on certain days and creates a visual timetable to help the children keep track of what day it is and to increase their visual literacy. She also wishes to use games more widely while the teaching assistant is more used to a traditional approach and worksheets.

The teaching assistant appears to set out to maintain her routines and countermands any strategy or system the teacher/student introduces. The large slide is brought out on days it should not be out and put away on days when the visual timetable says it should be out. She dismisses games as only fit for after the real work has been done and continues to use worksheets which have been squirrelled away for many years.

The tension between the two is palpable and the children start to suffer as well.

Consider: What is the real problem here?

How would you manage it if you found yourself in this situation?

Is there anyone else you could ask to help or advise you?

Where and how to use your teaching assistant

Learning support assistants can perform the following functions when working directly with children.

- Keep children on task by frequent reminders to return to work.
- Interpret information for children so that the child can continue working.
- Act as a facilitator in group tasks or talk situations.
- Facilitate thinking about a particular problem or aspect.
- Monitor behaviour in a group.
- Smooth social relations between certain children.
- Conduct informal 'on the spot' assessments.
- Give immediate feedback to children.
- Provide support and make connections across the curriculum for some children.
- Provide moral and emotional support for children.

REFLECTIVE TASK

Categorise the above activities, and add a few of your own, into surface activity, which is low-level engagement and understanding, or deep meaningful activity, which is a high level of engagement and understanding.

Now consider which you have seen most evidence of in classes you have been in. Different schools have different systems for supporting pupils with learning difficulties.

The main provisions involve a teaching assistant working as follows.

1. In class with a group of children in the main class, usually the low-ability group.
2. With a group but also cruising the room helping all children.
3. Taking a group of children (again usually the lower-ability children) out for an hour or so.
4. Taking individual children out for specific tuition.

You can also subdivide these groups into the type of work (differentiation) being undertaken: often the lower-ability group may have completely different work from the rest of the class, less often they may be working on something similar but with extra support. Dyslexic children more often do not need different work but just for it to be presented or explained differently or for extra thinking time to be allowed.

Lower ability or lower achieving

Lower-ability grouping is different from lower-achieving. Lower-achieving children may be achieving at a level which is not consistent with other indicators of ability. This group might include dyslexic children, dyspraxic children, ADHD children, gifted and talented children who have a specific learning difficulty and the potential to achieve more. Lower achieving suggests there is something you can do about the achievement because their actual ability is quite high. Describing a group as the low-ability group suggests there is something inherent in the children and that their achievement level is consistent with their ability level, i.e., they are achieving as best they can even though this may be low. You should be cautious therefore in how you group your children; you may want to cater for both of these groups as they will have different needs and you may certainly want to be thoughtful about the way you refer to them when speaking to other professionals. Ofsted (1999) makes comment on the practice of grouping pupils by reading deficit indicating that you may well group dyslexic pupils along with global learning difficulties pupils and you may limit the potential for achievement of dyslexic pupils by doing this.

You may also want to move children in and out of the lower-achieving group according to which subject is being tackled. Many dyslexic children may be low achieving in writing but not reading, they may be low achieving in English but good at mathematics or science. This again is noted by Ofsted (1999). This aspect highlights the importance of specific assessments and individual profiles being undertaken.

In-class support or withdrawal group?

You also need to consider what you want to achieve and the learning needs of your pupils. Dyslexic, dyspraxic and ADHD children have difficulty with concentration. While there is a political agenda for in-class support, often these children gain far more by being removed from the class for short specific teaching sessions. The general melée of the classroom can prove too distracting for them. It is important however, that if they are taken out, anything they may have missed is then taught or supported. Again your teaching assistant can help with this.

You should be aware that if your groups of children are withdrawn at certain times for extra tuition they do not miss subjects which might be considered 'less important' such as art, PE or music as these are subjects that these children may well perform well in and be able to feel some sense of achievement. Nor should they miss the same lesson each week. It is quite feasible to rotate withdrawal groups and this was achieved by careful record-keeping in one school ensuring that the children were rotated through a 3-group withdrawal programme. This meant that the child who missed 9 o'clock to 10 o'clock on week one would move to the 10 o'clock to 11 o'clock slot in week 2 and would miss break time but they would then move to the 11 o'clock to 12 o'clock slot the next week. This is perfectly possible with careful planning and record-keeping.

You may even consider swapping teaching assistants if you have certain assistants with different talents in different classes; some assistants may be more comfortable supporting mathematics than literacy. There is no ruling that one teaching assistant has to stay with a particular class/child all the time. It may be convenient for you to arrange your timetable with another teacher/student so that you both benefit from the expertise and skills of two teaching assistants.

Teaching assistants are often timetabled for morning sessions for literacy and numeracy. There is a good argument for placing these two subjects in the morning because children may be at their brightest then, but what implicit message is this giving about the rest of the curriculum where support may be equally needed for children with learning difficulties? It might be a good idea to swap lessons occasionally so that your learning support assistant can support music or history with children with dyslexia.

At the end of the day you should review activities with your teaching assistant. You convey your impression of what they have been doing and vice versa. Don't just assume that what they have done has all gone well and that they are happy with being just used. If you ignore your teaching assistant you risk devaluing what they do.

Not everything in the garden is rosy

While the benefits of working with teaching assistants cannot be ignored, nor can the challenges. Wilson et al. (2007) report that the use of TAs can lead to lower workloads, particularly in freeing up staff for PPA time: however the evaluation of the pilot study (Wilson et al., 2003) and surveys undertaken by the teaching unions indicate that this is not always the case. Supervision of, and liaison with, other adults can add to the overall workload and stress of teachers. There can be tensions between teacher and TA if the relationship does not work well. There can be lack of clarity of responsibilities and sensitivities may be trampled on if one character has overwhelming strengths or a particularly strong character. There also needs to be accord when dealing with a third person in the room such as a student. It would be counterproductive all round for the student to receive two sets of conflicting instructions. All of these situations can be eased if there are clear communications between all parties, honesty, respect and integrity. If you are organised and respect the skills of your TA they are likely to be more tolerant of your occasional weaknesses. You need to make your TA feel valued and needed. Too often TAs feel taken for granted or not valued enough. You need to recognise the worth of your TA and to let them know how much you appreciate their support and make them feel valued at all times. Nothing develops this more than a good list of tasks you would like them to support you with. Being at a loose end engenders lack of motivation and tedium, and will in the end demotivate your TA.

PRACTICAL TASK PRACTICAL TASK PRACTICAL TASK PRACTICAL TASK **PRACTICAL TASK**

Draw up a list of different tasks you consider it would be useful for your TA to support you with. These may be tasks you consider they are more skilled at than you are, or they may be a division of labour which has been agreed. It should not be a delegation of the messiest and most mundane jobs in the class. There have been some excellent TAs who have taken umbrage at being left to wash the paint pots every week when they felt they could be better used developing resources or filing documentation. Having drawn up a 'possibilities' list, sit down and discuss this list with your TA on your next placement. When you have done this, pin up the list in your classroom. This can then form a plan of action for any time when your TA finds they have spare time on their hands. Your TA should not feel that you can manage without them once the lesson activities have finished and they should not feel that they are wasting time in your class.

Make a list of the skills acquired from outside school which your TA could use in your class. Some TAs may be able to touch-type and would be excellent for supporting a child using a computer who needs keyboard skills. Get to know your TA and find out what their hidden skills and hobbies are.

Being aware of stigmatism and difference

Although it is your responsibility to support your children with any special needs, you do need to be aware of the impact of your actions and the effect of your support generally. It is easy to support a child academically but to also create a forum for difference being highlighted rather than just accepted. Your use of your teaching assistant is crucial in this and this is where you may wish to use a variety of support contexts and different strategies to spread the opportunities for support; Ofsted (1999) noted that often the strategies used for learning-difficulties children were used to the benefit of all children in the class. This is when good practice with children with SEN is good practice for all children, and it is also a more productive use of your TA. Your TA probably does not need to sit with one child all the time; they could support other children and draw the child they are assisting into the circle of other children. This is particularly important for children who are allocated a TA for social and emotional reasons rather than learning support. It is also of benefit at the end of Key Stage 2 if a TA who has been supporting a child such as a Down's syndrome child needs to step back to allow them a little social independence ready for Key Stage 3. They could well support a child who is in need of support but who does not have their own TA allocated to them.

You need to be aware of this in the type of activity and work you provide to your dyslexic pupils, the support you afford them, the expected level of work and how you respond to their work. At what point does recognition of the efforts and difficulties of dyslexic children convey to other children that some people can produce work that is less than what is expected from others? Why is it acceptable that other children should strive for correct spelling whereas for some children you will accept an element of misspelling? Your teaching assistant needs to be equally aware of these issues and you need to work together to combat any perceptions of dyslexic children getting better attention or being allowed to produce substandard work. This will be evident in how and when you use your teaching assistant and for which tasks. It is suggested you have a strategy to combat any discrimination, such as if one group of children is taken out at a certain time for particular teaching you do the same for other groups in rotation. This withdrawal may be for different subjects, not just literacy. Dyslexic children may be withdrawn for help with numeracy and literacy but other groups could equally be withdrawn for science or art. The effect though is to convey to all children that they are all equally entitled to group support and provided with the same opportunities.

Some ideal activities for teaching assistants

Screening children

Teaching assistants, particularly those who have taken short courses in identifying 'at risk' children such as those advertised at www.classroom-assistant.net/ or provided through organisations such as DyslexiaAction, are ideal in carrying out the initial screening of children. The activities listed earlier (Chapter 2) can easily be undertaken by a teaching assistant who can then discuss the results with you for further referral.

ICT

The use of the computer is a widely recognised support for dyslexic children; however, there are skills embedded in the use of ICT, particularly the use of a spell checker and filing documents as well as keyboard skills. Ofsted (1999) noted that pupils who *learned keyboard skills were the most successful at using word processing programs to assist them in their writing.* It takes repetition and patient questioning when children have forgotten how to use these facilities. The use of a teaching assistant sitting between two children using computers is a great use of their time. It develops independence in the learner and releases you to concentrate on the rest of the class. This can be applied to mathematics games as well.

TAs can equally adapt the screen resolution and font to suit the needs of children. Hand-held spell checkers need a certain level of knowledge and understanding before they can be used successfully. Your TA can sit with small groups and tutor them in the technicalities of using them.

Creating activities and games

Once your TA has taken some training they will know appropriate ways of teaching dyslexic children and where likely problems may arise. If you inform them of the outcomes you wish to achieve they are the ideal person to create games and activities specifically for the children they work with. They are equally the best person to adapt work activities, if they have been alert to what children have been telling them they should know what is needed.

Making audio recordings on tape and MP3 players

One of the best supports for dyslexic children learning to read is a good model of reading to follow and to hear a text being read. Your teaching assistant could read texts onto an audio recorder for your dyslexic children to play for themselves. This could even be used as a group activity if you have multiple earphones to one tape machine. By recording the reading onto tape it allows you or your teaching assistant to observe the children while they are listening to the reading rather than looking at the book. Equivalent texts using story boards on the computer can also be created.

Extra reading sessions

For many dyslexic children an area of deficit is lack of 'hearing' language and stories read. Because literacy has been a struggle for them or because their concentration is limited, they may not have benefited as much as other children from story sessions. Opportunities to listen to and engage in story response sessions are greater in small groups with a teaching assistant who can focus on individual responses and draw particular children into the story. Some children are also more likely to speak out in small groups than in the whole-class context. The same applies to mathematics activities and games.

Making games

You may have an idea to make learning more fun but be pushed for time to make individual games. If you discuss this idea with your teaching assistant, not only might you devise a better game between you but they can also make the game which they can then play with the children. Making the game gives them a better understanding of the game and its pitfalls. You will be truly involving your teaching assistant at all levels in this way. This is supported by Wilson et al. (2007) with regard to developing new ideas.

Supervising self-check games

Many of the games suggested in this book can be played by children in small groups but often there is a need for an adult to make sure that the rules are being observed or that the game is being played in the right way. Teaching assistants can also raise the level of academic input into these games or adapt them laterally if they are understanding and creative.

Supporting writing

Many dyslexic children have difficulty writing for a number of reasons and you will find further details on the difficulties of writing in the chapter on writing (Chapter 5). Your teaching assistant may be the best person to:

- sit and tease ideas out of a child who appears to have nothing to say;
- draft with the child using pictures, photographs or audio logs;
- check the height of the table/chair and provide suitable resources to address this;
- organise the angle of the paper and stick it down;
- correct the pencil grip of a child;
- correct letter formation of a child;
- read and reread so that the child keeps on track with their writing;
- take turns with the child in scribing what the child wants to say;
- help the child to organise and edit their work.

Too often the teaching assistant is given no clear guidance on how to help children with writing difficulties and is just a prompt to keep on task. You need to inform your teaching assistant of exactly what you want and help them to carry out their role.

Observations

Very often to move forward with children with learning difficulties you need to observe them for a while to find out where their difficulties lie. In situations such as whole-class input sessions such as at the start of the literacy or numeracy session, your teaching assistant is the ideal person to observe and make notes of responses from certain children. You are probably too engrossed in actually teaching and making sure you follow your plan to note all the information that pupils will provide during this time.

Supporting children during the literacy or numeracy session

Often a teaching assistant is assigned to specific children and will sit with them during the whole-class input of the literacy session. These teaching assistants can act as a partner or as another child would in paired talk sessions or when children are asked to discuss ideas. Too often a pair of children where one is dyslexic (or any other SEN) will not talk or keep on track because the concentration of one is limited and it is beyond the scope of the other child to keep things moving. In this instance the teaching assistant can either sit with the pair or replace a child.

A teaching assistant can also repeat, rephrase or clarify topics under discussion or text being read for a dyslexic child.

Early literacy support, *additional literacy support* and *further literacy support* have been designed to help failing children and while they include a good number of resources and activities to use, these are not aimed specifically at dyslexic children nor the needs of a particular child. Your teaching assistant who is familiar with these packages should be able to adapt them to the needs of individual pupils or groups of pupils. Similarly, the *Springboard* materials need to be customised, as does any commercially produced material.

Completing daily logs and parent diaries

The teaching assistant who works with dyslexic children most of the time is in the best position to provide comments, feedback and suggestions to parents. They can also chat with the child at greater length than you will have time for, about their perceptions of reading and writing and feed into the holistic information about the child.

Emotional support sessions

It is important not to overlook the social and emotional aspects of dyslexia. It is easy to focus on the academic only. Many dyslexic children have low self-esteem and feelings of lack of self-worth. It is important to counter these as early as possible.

It may be necessary to involve parents in informal support group work because sometimes these feelings are inadvertently created at home by insensitive remarks such as *well you can't spell anyway* or *I was always useless at school too*. While these comments are not meant maliciously, they embed within self-image and can last into adult life. Similarly, parents might need support in coming to terms with how a dyslexic child fits into the family, especially if the dyslexic child is an older child. It is very difficult to manage when younger children start to be more capable than an older child in literacy activities. Some siblings may need support as well. It is not uncommon for brothers and sisters to feel guilty that they have no disability and have an easier life than their dyslexic sibling. Equally there may be feelings of resentment because a dyslexic child gets so much attention and support, and this can then lead to feelings of guilt. Your teaching assistant may be a much better person to engage in these activities than you would be.

REFLECTIVE TASK

How many different teaching assistants have you come into contact with? Were they included in the preparation of tasks and consulted on what specific children required? Were they free to make games, etc.? Consider how you could include a TA in the support for one particular child. What implications does this have for your planning and forward preparation?

A SUMMARY OF **KEY POINTS**

> Teaching assistants come in many guises – be clear about what type of teaching assistant you have and what type you want.

> Teaching assistants need guidance and continuing professional development in order to support you and the children fully.

> Teaching assistants may be more specialised than you in some areas but you are always the person who has the final responsibility for the children in your class.

> Swop activities so that all children benefit from support in different lessons.

> Monitor withdrawal sessions so that the same subject is not missed by the same group each week.

> You should liaise with your teaching assistant daily so that everyone is clear as to what is expected of them.

> Without being patronising, congratulate your teaching assistant and thank them for their contribution – we all like to be appreciated.

MOVING *ON* > > > > > > MOVING *ON* > > > > > > MOVING *ON*

Examine the Standards for QTS and note how many of them are directly linked or could be linked to the use of teaching assistants.

In the considered use of your teaching assistant, what evidence would you collect to demonstrate that you have met these standards?

REFERENCES REFERENCES **REFERENCES** REFERENCES **REFERENCES** REFERENCES

Burden, B (2005) *Dyslexia and self concept: seeking a dyslexic identity.* London: Whurr Publishing

DfES (2000) *Working with teaching assistants.* London: HMSO

Hall, W (2004) Inclusion: special needs, in Bold, C (ed.) *Supporting learning and teaching.* London: David Fulton

Hall, W (2005) Making the most of the teaching assistant for special educational needs, in Campbell, A and Fairbairn, G (2005) *Working with support in the classroom.* London: Paul Chapman Publishing

Ofsted (1999) *Pupils with specific learning difficulties in mainstream schools.* London: HMSO

Ofsted (2004) *Special educational needs and disability: towards inclusive schools.* London: Ofsted

Ofsted (2005) *Ofsted subject reports 2003/04 English in primary schools HMI 2413.* London: HMSO 2005

Ryan, A, Pintrich, P and Midgley, C (2001) Avoiding seeking help in the classroom: who and why?. *Educational Psychology Review*, 13 (2): 93–114

Savage, R and Carless, S (2005) Learning support assistants and effective reading interventions for 'at-risk' children. *Educational Research*, 47(1): 45-61

The Times Educational Supplement (staffroom) online 1 March 2008 www.tes.co.uk/section/staffroom/thread.aspx?story_id=2584827&path=/teaching+assistants/&threadPage=1&messagePage=1 (accessed 4/3/2008)

Wilson, V, Schlapp, U and Davidson, J (2003) Insight 1: Classroom assistants: key issues from the National Evaluation, cited by Hall, W (2005) Making the most of the teaching assistant for special educational needs, in Campbell, A and Fairbairn, G *Working with support in the classroom.* London: Paul Chapman Publishing

Wilson, R, Sharp, C, Shuayb, M, Kendall, L, Wade, P and Easton, C (2007) *Research into the deployment and impact of support staff who have achieved HLTA status. Final Report.* Slough: NFER

Useful website

Classroom assistant at www.classroom-assistant.net/

4
Teaching spelling: games and activities

Chapter objectives

By the end of this chapter you should be aware of:

- **the skills necessary to teach spelling and different ways of learning aspects of spelling;**
- **the difficulties many dyslexic children encounter in trying to learn our complicated language;**
- **a variety of games and activities which will enhance the teaching and learning of core skills to improve children's ability to spell.**

This chapter addresses the following Professional Standards for QTS:

Q10, Q12, Q14, Q17, Q19, Q22, Q23, Q25(a), (b), (c), (d), Q26b.

Introduction

The ability to spell is often viewed as the mark of an educated person. The ability to spell is often used as a benchmark. Poor spelling may, mistakenly, convey the impression of lack of education or intelligence. After handwriting, it is the first thing that strikes you about a piece of writing. Poor spelling often impedes the ability to read the meaning and is a barrier to effective communication.

The ability to spell is not only important in creating a piece of writing, it is also crucial to and informs the reading process. If you can spell a word you can generally read it, although the reverse is not always true. It is quite common to be able to read a word but not spell it. The English language is particularly difficult since there are over 200 rules with 45 exceptions and little guidance on when to apply the rule and when to apply the exception. Dyslexia is more prevalent in languages that are less regular in their spelling. While the focus of this chapter is on spelling and more often than not a dyslexic person may have difficulty with spelling, this is not always true. It is quite possible to find a dyslexic person who has adequate spelling strategies but has great difficulty in reading or in mathematics. For those of you teaching children who do display real difficulties with spelling, I hope the following games and activities are useful.

Theoretical background

Spelling is one of the areas most dyslexic children, and adults, have considerable difficulty with. Spelling (encoding) is an almost reciprocal activity to reading (decoding), so many of the suggestions in the reading section can be mirrored here. I say 'almost' because it is not exactly the opposite. Encoding is automatically more difficult because you have a blank page to work on with few clues whereas at least with decoding you have the word in front of you and, if you are reading holistically, some clues to help you. If you are grappling with the difficulties of spelling you are usually, as a child, also grappling with the complexities of sentence construction, possibly handwriting and keeping your work in some sort of order on the page. Montgomery (2000) notes that very able and gifted children who have dyslexia may read well but may be hampered by very poor spelling. Because learning support is usually linked to reading age, these children may never receive the tuition they need or they may be referred later than their peers. She notes one child of 15 who has a spelling age of 6.8 years whose Individual Education Plan focuses solely on his reading capabilities. Pollock and Waller (2001) also state that *although reading has always been given more prominence than spelling in the early days at school, spelling in fact poses the greater problem for dyslexic children and this difficulty can continue long after the reading difficulty has been greatly improved* (p49).

This chapter does not outline the various theories of spelling, as there are many excellent textbooks which do that together with formal instruction of how to introduce various rules (for example, Ott, 1997; Pollock and Waller, 2001). Ehri (2005) and Hornsby (1995) argue for the introduction of phonic tuition before word recognition tuition, as does the Primary National Strategy. However, many feel that the question of whether visual strategies or phonics comes first depends on the profile that pupils present through assessment especially as some dyslexic children will encounter failure through phonic strategies; this being their weakest domain. Formative and diagnostic assessment are important in achieving QTS Standards 12 and 26a. It can be argued that dyslexic children need both phonics and look and say as well as contextual understanding, in differing proportions, right from the start and certainly by the time they are evidencing failure in school. This view was supported by the Cox Report (1989) when the National Curriculum was introduced, and has since been reported by other researchers who put forward the theory of the graphemic output lexicon being integral to the ability to spell (Giles and Terrell, 1997). Goswami and Ziegler (2006) also assert that phonology and orthography are intimately connected from the beginning of reading.

This chapter examines the difficulties most dyslexic children encounter with spelling and suggests strategies to help children learn spellings through visual routes and through phonics.

The routes to learning spelling

The two main avenues to spelling are auditory strategies (phonics) and visual strategies (look and say), each having a set of sub-skills upon which the whole skill rests. Most good spellers use a combination of strategies, and adult spellers rely predominantly on memory, visual and physio-motor memory. The current philosophy in reading, of phonics first, foremost and fast (DfES, 2007), may suit some children but it will do little to assist many dyslexic children who have huge difficulties with phonics, unless that programme is adapted to the specific needs of those children and complemented by other material suitable to their profile of strengths and weaknesses. To promote one method of teaching and learning over others is to deny the research regarding individual learning, multiple intelligences and subgroups of dyslexia. Furthermore, the ability to read assists the ability to spell. Children will very often be able to spell words they can read. Children who experience difficulty with phonics will experience the 'double deficit' with a predominantly phonics programme.

The importance of assessing and determining the learning profile of the children you work with cannot be stressed too strongly. Some dyslexic children will have difficulties mainly with phonics and be relatively strong with visual strategies of look and say; others may have the reverse profile and have considerable weaknesses in the visual domain, having difficulties with sequencing and orientation but may have some strengths with phonics; more commonly children will have difficulties with both of these, having a relative strength in one and more difficulty with the other but neither being such a strength as to be relied on completely. Pumfrey and Reason (1997) noted that the only advantage to identifying subtypes is if some curricular advantage follows, such as an adapted teaching schedule tailored to their subtype, which is not typically the case. Today it should be the case and this book is based on the premise that subtype is important in defining how we teach dyslexic children.

When teaching dyslexic children it is important to address both their strength and their weakness. Their strength can be used to teach them certain spellings and to boost their confidence. It is motivating for children to have a list of spellings they know they can spell rather than a long list of words they cannot spell. It is also necessary to address their weakness so that they are not permanently disadvantaged and can use more than one strategy. You will find some teachers either only address the weakness, ignoring the strength, or others who only address the strength, believing you cannot 'remedy' the weakness of dyslexia. Both these positions can be detrimental to the child, ignoring the fact that children can develop new learning skills and that learning patterns can change over time and with different activities.

Remember that the visual route is the direct route and when this works well it gives direct access to words that are stored and instantly retrieved. This, coupled with the auto-motor activity of writing, is how most adult spellers arrive at a quick and mostly accurate spelling of a word. Unfortunately, many dyslexic children have poor visual memory and will need extra support and practice to learn spellings visually. The normal 'look, cover, write, check' strategy that may work for most children will not be sufficient and may even be demotivating for dyslexic children if they do not learn by this process. Multisensory teaching is much more than this very basic imitation. Multisensory teaching should involve not just all of the senses but should involve movement both large and small. The phonics route is the indirect route and requires more in terms of processing, which is why children with poor working memory experience the 'double deficit'. It can be useful for a child who has no idea of how a word should look, but our language is not phonetically regular. Even the Primary National Strategy (DfES, 2007), with its focus on phonics, admits there are 'tricky words' which need to be learnt visually. In this chapter the activities which will help with learning rules will develop automaticity and provide practice for all children without resorting to the over-use of worksheets and repetitive spelling lists. These activities will help you develop the core literacy skills of your pupils and help you to achieve QTS standard 23. Dyslexic children need more practice than non-dyslexic children but it needs to be motivating, enjoyable and require them to think as well. The activities and games suggested provide all of this. It is a 'bottom up' model, as noted by Porter (2002), who states that:

> rather than attempting to instil a predetermined curriculum, the bottom up approach respects and responds reflectively to the skills and interests of children and their parents. However it does not simply indulge these or rely on improvisation or chance, it utilises educators' expertise and active teaching while engaging children's (and parents') competence. (p58)

While children are playing and engaged they are motivated; the more they play the more practice they are getting and, depending on how you structure the game or activity, they are often required to think and make informed choices about how to proceed. Rather than minor variations of drills and practices, the games here provide children with opportunities to enjoy the task and become immersed in the playing of the game rather than the learning of the rule. This personalising of learning helps you meet QTS standards 10 and 19.

When you write words, you use visual memory as the primary avenue of checking the word and then use other strategies to assist or confirm this first route. You write automatically, you may then think *that doesn't look right*; at this point you are using your visual memory. You may try other variations checking against visual memory. You may then resort to other techniques such as sounding parts of the word out, using syllable division or mnemonics to help you.

Using games to develop spelling skills

Principles for playing games

- Build on what children already know.
- Teach, practise and play, with rules or spelling patterns in a systematic way.
- Introduce new rules or patterns in a cumulative way.
- Use multisensory techniques as much as possible to reinforce your main mode of teaching
- Relate the teaching of spelling to and reinforce it in your tuition of reading and writing.

Hints for using game cards

- Children with dyslexia may also be dyspraxic, experiencing manipulation difficulties. Wind rubber bands around the edge of playing cards in order to give extra grip.
- Make the cards just large enough to fit into the hands of the children you are teaching. If you make the cards too small they will get screwed up but if you make them too large the child is likely to drop them.
- Some children may need matt lamination to minimise glare. If you cannot get matt you could spray your cards with hairspray – when this dries it leaves a matt finish.
- Use at least 14 point bold text, preferably dark brown or blue in colour on cream-coloured card. This addresses the needs of both dyslexic children and children with scotopic sensitivity syndrome, which is often co-morbid with dyslexia.
- Always recap on previous games and learning before moving on or build in a review section to games.

REFLECTIVE TASK

Think about your most recent placement.

What prior learning was activated in the lessons you were engaged in or did you just assume children would remember how to make connections? Make sure you take time to check what children remember before moving on.

How many different strategies were active in any one lesson to support spelling using a variety of methods?

Phonics games

The ability to spell with phonics involves several sub-skills. These include the ability to:

- hear discrete sounds or phonemes;
- replicate these sounds and to sequence them in a remembered pattern;

- deconstruct a word into its constituent phonemes;
- split words into syllables and 'hear' the pattern in words;
- match the sound (phoneme) to a letter (grapheme);
- combine several patterns that have been learnt such as combining digraphs into a whole word.

If a child is not hearing sounds and reproducing them accurately, they will have difficulty with phonics regardless of whether they are dyslexic or not. This assumes the child's hearing has already been investigated and some of the screening tasks suggested in earlier chapters have been carried out indicating there is nothing to suggest that the child should be referred for medical intervention such as grommets. The following activities will develop their ability to hear sounds and to think about sounds. They provide practice and repeated opportunities to think about sounds while the child is playing and having fun.

Game 1: Same and different

Aim: to support the ability to hear different sounds
This is an activity straight from the National Literacy Strategy; many of you may already be familiar with it.

Resources required: a bag of items such as doll, ball, bat, cat, pen, hen, (playing) card, pin.

How to play: Easy version
Hold the bag in front of you but with the top open just enough to allow a hand to enter.

Ask the child to take two items from the bag, say their names and state whether the items start with the same or different sounds (phonemes). Because of the chance of getting two the same this game can be endless and you may want to move to the teacher-led version.

How to play: Teacher-led version
Select the items from the bag for the child to consider.

You may choose 'bat' and 'cat' and ask the child if the words start with the same sound. The child has to respond with *same* or *different*.

If they are correct they can keep those items; if incorrect the items go back in the bag.

Game 2: Simon says

Aim: to support the ability to hear sounds
This is a variation of the well known game of Simon says but it focuses on children hearing sounds and obeying a command.

Resources required: none

How to play
You might say for example, "Simon says everyone whose name begins with the sound sssss sit down." If necessary this can be modified to give an example: "*everyone whose names start with sssss, like Sally, sit down.*"

Harder version matching phoneme to grapheme

Resources required: a set of alphabet letters (graphemes)

How to play
Play in the same way as for the first version but extend by showing the grapheme of the letter as the phoneme is said or not saying the phoneme at all but letting the children say the phoneme as you show the grapheme.

Observe children who give incorrect answers, praise the children giving correct answers and give them a grapheme card to collect – you automatically then have a recording system for the children who know the correspondence.

All this requires is the ingenuity of the teacher in constructing instructions for different phonemes and their place in words. The variations are names that start with, end with or have the sound in them.

Game 3: Alliteration games
Aim: to support the ability to hear sounds
The ability to provide another sound the same is crucial and probably the best indicator of whether a child is hearing and identifying a sound. This activity can be used as a way of dismissing children in an orderly manner at break time and home time.

Resources required: none

How to play:
Start by giving a demonstration of names and words that start the same way. *I want you to think of a word that starts the same way as your name, so I might ask Mandy to find a word that starts with the same sound as her name, a word like messy or marvellous. These words all start with the mmm sound that is at the start of Mandy's name.*

You then give the children a minute or two to think of a word or ask certain children.

Again alphabet cards could be held up at the same time or the teacher could ask the child to find the letter from a display on the wall to extend and consolidate this knowledge.

Those children left at the end would be those who you then need to focus on in a smaller group to explicitly teach and develop acuity of hearing. A variation on this could be for you to provide alliterative or non-alliterative pairs and for the child to say whether this was correct or not and if not can they provide a pair?

Game 4: Picture snap
Aim: to support the ability to hear sounds
A game similar to the above but using the game of snap.

Resources required: a set of picture cards, home-made or you could use those supplied at the back of the folder *Early Literacy Support* from the National Literacy Strategy.

How to play
Deal the cards.

Play snap where each player places a card alternately on the pile.

Players have to say whether the word that goes with the picture starts with the same sound as the previous card.

Correct answers – the child collects the pile.

Incorrect answers – you use this as a teaching opportunity to draw attention to the difference.

Variations
To make this a bit more even, if you play you will generally get this right, introduce the rule that sometimes you might make mistakes and the child can win by spotting your mistakes. In this way the child can not only win by identifying their own snaps and saying the phoneme but by being attentive and spotting when you have snapped two cards which don't start with the same phoneme. Switch to end phonemes for variation. Be sure of the words that go with each card before playing this game. A pond could just as easily be a lake, a shed could easily be a hut; so you might get incorrect responses not because the child cannot identify sounds but because they are thinking of a different word.

Game 5: Phoneme bingo
Aim: to support the ability to match phoneme to grapheme
This is an easy variation on the game of bingo.

Resources required: baseboards with about six graphemes on each board
Tiles bearing graphemes of chosen letters for teaching/assessing.

How to play
You can play in several ways.

Play with picture cards.

C	t	H
F	c	B

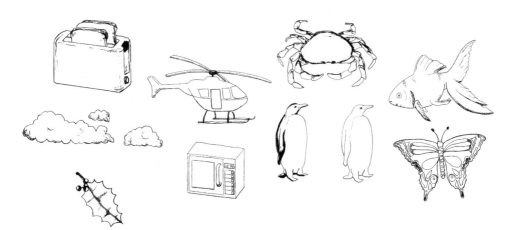

Players match the initial phoneme/grapheme on the board to the word which corresponds to their pictures. This is similar to the game of snap above but introduces the grapheme for them to match. Vary it by focusing on final consonant as well, for which you will need to make a new baseboard. It is essential that you do not provide them with the written letter to match to the letters on the baseboard because it then becomes a visual exercise. This latter activity is valid if you are developing visual skills but not for developing phonic skills.

It is advisable to have at least one or two cards that don't fit into the grid. This prevents children just placing cards with little thought, you can also have more than one place for a grapheme to reinforce certain letters and sounds.

Game 6: Bingo scrabble
Aim: to support the ability to match phoneme to grapheme

Resources required: same as above

How to play
This game is similar to bingo but can be used when children need to speed up in their recognition.

Give each child a baseboard and place all of the picture cards on the table.

Give the children a minute to collect as many of the picture cards as they can to match their board.

Get each child to check another child's board for accuracy.

The winner is not just the child who was quickest but also who has the most correct.

Game 7: Ladders
Aim: to support the ability to match phoneme to grapheme
This game is similar to bingo but uses ladders to win the game. This game teaches medial vowels. You need picture cards of objects with easy medial vowels. Again be careful of the pictures you chose: a hen could be a chicken, which would complicate the game.

Your baseboard is a ladder with about six rungs on it.

You need a sticky spot on the bottom of your ladder where you stick a grapheme. Leaving the baseboard 'open' allows adaptation of the game and more versatility, even the possibility of teaching tables by altering the symbol at the bottom of the ladder. When you have chosen the vowel for each child to collect, place the picture cards face down on the table. Each child takes a turn to select a card. If they have a card that contains an object whose name has the vowel to go with their board they place that card on the bottom rung of their ladder. If it is not their vowel they put the card back down. You can encourage the children to watch and remember where cards that they might want have been placed. The winner is the one to collect cards and reach the top of their ladder first.

Variations
You can give a child more vowels so that they concentrate on several vowels and select between them. To start with you can allow them to collect their vowels in any order to get to the top of the ladder. Later on you can stipulate an order that they must collect them in.

Game 8: Medial vowel bingo
Aim: to develop the ability to hear and match medial vowels with graphemes
This game is a variation of the well-known bingo game but on the baseboard you write words with a medial vowel missing. On your play cards you have your vowels of a, i, o, u and e.

Resources required: baseboard, tiles bearing vowels.
Your baseboard may look like this:

c_t	r_n	f_n	p_g	p_n	h_n
d_g	t_p	p_t	b_g	l_g	m_n

How to play
Turn the vowels face down on the table.

Children turn a tile over to try to make a word.

They say the vowel and word, if incorrect they return the tile.

You will notice that the words have several possibilities, there is not one right answer; you could have run or ran, fan or fin , tip or top, pit, pat or pet or even put (although this would be a step up at this stage because this is not a phonic word because the *u* says a different sound in 'put' to 'pub'), you could have man or men, leg or log.

Variation
Once the children are competent with short medial phonemes you could introduce them to long medial vowel and the use of final *e* to modify the vowel. It is suggested you use a red-coloured 'e' for teaching the rule of final e modifying the medial vowel as a variation. You would have to select your vowels and words carefully or play it such that the child identifies which words are open to this change. Cut to cute works but cat to cate does not. You need to be thoughtful and selective about the letters you choose for each variation of the game.

Visual strategies/look and say games

Visual recognition is the basis for automatic spelling and reading. This is often the check of whether we think a word is spelt correctly as well. It is visual recognition that makes words such as 'elephant' and 'aeroplane' memorable for many young children because they have a distinctive visual outline. However, many children who are dyslexic have a poor memory for sequence and orientation and many words are visually similar. Children need to be able to recognise both the general sequence of letters in words and also pay attention to fine details in words. The following games improve the ability to remember visual detail. This will then help children to remember spellings when they are learning them by pattern rather than by phonically building them up.

Game 1: 'Challenge me' memory game
Aim: to develop visual memory for sequence

Resources required: a set of picture cards. You can cut pictures out of magazines or use a web-based programme or if you are creative take photographs yourself.

How to play
Start by challenging the child to say how many pictures they think they can remember in the correct sequence. Most children estimate about six.

Tell them you are going to show (avoid the word 'teach' because this seems to have a switch-off effect with many children) them a way in which they will be able to remember up to 25 in a few weeks.

Start by placing around five or six cards in a sequence, show first one card and place it down then turn over the next card and place it next to the first and so on until you have five or six cards in a line.

Allow the child 30 seconds to look at the cards and then remove them in the exact order you placed them down.

Ask the child to say what the cards were in the correct order.

If they are right, praise them and ask them how they did it; some children have already devised their own strategy.

If they have no strategy, challenge them to remember two more cards next time and ask if they would like to know a special way that would help them.

Most primary children are keen to know 'special ways'. Tell them that as you show them the pictures they are to create a story around the picture, it doesn't matter how silly or fantastic the story is because it is only for them. It is like making a video in the brain.

Now place the first five or six cards down and add two more.

Ask the child to rerun their video in their brain before you remove the cards.

Now remove the cards and ask the child to name them in the correct order. Most children are fascinated by this technique, which is commonly used by memory men; the technique is called embedding.

If the child achieves the new goal of seven or more, challenge them to remember two more. Each time they retell the core story and add to it. You may need to check early on whether they are really weaving a story or just listing the cards. Listing does not work; it is the act of creating a story which the child can remember which is significant in this activity.

Always stop with success, if they fail with increased cards return to the last success and rerun this so that they finish having achieved.

Each session add two more cards with each run.

Every so often shuffle the cards so that they have to create a new story. Soon the child will remember anything in the region of 25-plus cards. They really enjoy telling their parents they can remember 25 cards and challenging their parents to do the same, which most often they cannot do.

Game 2: Variations on Kim's game

Aim: to develop strategies to aid visual recall

This game develops the ability to organise learning and visual memory. Most children know Kim's game, where a tray bearing several items is placed in front of you to remember or identify what has been moved.

Resources required: a variety of items such as paper clip, eraser, button, cotton-reel, screw, crayon, key, small bauble, gift tag (allow the child to select some of the items to go on the tray and you select the rest).

Start with a manageable number such as 12.

How to play

Show the child how to organise the items in some sort of a pattern so that they are not just randomly all over the tray. Different ways of organising may include colour, size, the material they are made from and the purpose of the object.

Once you have established the sorting category, the child places the items into groups.

Now organise them again in some order, perhaps in rank order to how many items are in each group. From a group of 12 items you may have 1 yellow item, 2 blue items, 4 green items, 5 red items.

Once organised, get the child to feel and say what is in each group, describe any significant features of the object, if they are sharp of if they are springy or squashy, etc. This is real multisensory teaching.

When you have done this with each group, tell the child to close their eyes and ask them to tell you how many items were in the green group, the yellow group and so on and what they were, when you have practised each group tell the child to have one last look.

Review any group that posed a difficulty.

Now remove all items and ask the child to systematically go through each group until they have replaced all items back on the table in the same order they were previously. Each time add another few items to the collection.

Rerun the game at least twice in each session. Each week add more items and every so often change the items completely. When you do this, reduce the items for a session or so.

Game 3: Minimal pairs
Aim: to improve the ability to remember small differences in words

Resources required
Words that are very similar. It is best played as a game between two children.

Here is a list to start you off.

Horse	house	Friend	fiend
Steal	steal	Blind	Bind
Band	Brand	String	Sting
Sand	Stand	Plane	plant

Cut these words into single cards of the same size.

How to play
Place all tiles face down on the table, show the children how to turn over two cards, if they have two exactly the same they keep the pair.

Often you have to draw their attention to small differences when they think they have a pair.

Children take turns to find a pair.

When a pair is found they say the word and keep that pair.

Play ends when all pairs have been matched and read.

In the first stages limit play to four words so that the chances of picking a pair are greater and the children get used to what they have to do. The children not only have to remember to look carefully at the words they have selected but when they have played this a few times they realise they can remember where someone else placed a card that would match one they picked up earlier. It is a good idea when playing this at a developed level to have one or two odd cards so that at the end they cannot just pick up the last two cards left. This technique can be applied to learning tables – I will address this in the chapter related to maths (Chapter 7).

Game 4: Nonsense bingo
Aim: to develop the ability to remember visual sequences

The focus in this activity is to look at the shape of word units. Use a nonsense alphabet rather than a familiar one or use non-words which are quite similar.

Encourage the children to focus on particular features of words and to notice order and orientation.

Resources required: a baseboard, tiles bearing nonsense words to play. (Wingdings is a good program to use for this.)

Your baseboard may look something like this:

℘℃ℨ❶	⑤❶❶	⑨℃ℨ❶	⑨℃ℨ⑤	℃ℨ⑨④	℘℃ℨ❶
℘℃ℨ⑤	④℃ℨ⑤	④℃ℨ❶	℘❶❶	℃ℨ℘❶	℘❶⑤

Or this:

trif	**tirf**	**golb**	**Gobl**	**firt**	**pleq**
qlep	**rfin**	**nifr**	**Frin**	**lbog**	**lpeq**

You need duplicates of the non-words. Start with easy three- or four-digit spans. As the children improve you can extend the span to four, five or six to really get them to concentrate. It is not recommended to use more than six as there is some evidence that it is difficult for most people to conserve beyond five when the pattern they are looking at makes no sense.

How to play
Hold up a card for five seconds only and then hide it.

Children have to find the identical one on their board.

The first child to complete their board accurately wins.

Variations
Fast bingo. Place all the cards face down on the table and allow the children one minute to find all the tiles that match their baseboard.

When finished get the children to check each other's boards.

Incorrect items return to the table to complete play.

The winner is not only the first to finish but the one with all tiles correct.

You can make this task harder by adding fake cards which are not on the boards at all; this really makes the children pay attention to detail.

With a photocopier you can make mirror images as well which increases the skill level. The ability to remember an order of letters and orientation is crucial in accurate spelling. Errors such as siad written in children's work are because they know the letters but cannot remember the precise order. Recognising this not just as a mistake but as a significant aspect of learning is important and helps you achieve QTS standards 12 and 26b.

Systematic teaching of rules and spelling patterns

You can use many of the activities outlined above to teach spelling patterns and rules and reinforce them in a fun way. You can make snap from word families where the child uses their understanding of word families to snap the cards. Or you can use rules snap, where they are looking at the rule of, for example, suffixing – whether the consonant is doubled or not and why. In this activity they would be only looking at the root word, for example the snap cards would be made up of words such as tip, tape, tap, give, run, jump, skip, and so on. They would use their knowledge to say whether two consecutive words doubled or not their final consonant when suffixed. This is quite high-level work and would not be recommended for beginning tuition.

CASE STUDY

Jemma was nine years old when presented to me by her class teacher. She was very good orally and could create texts using a tape recorder or if given a writer to help her, but left on her own, her writing was almost undecipherable. Sometimes she would play safe with words she knew she could spell but then her writing was so simplistic that she was unhappy with the result and other children commented on how babyish it was. She was not often included in group writing activities because of this. Each week she received a reduced list of spellings from the class list. She would remember some of the class spellings but not all. She had good phonic abilities but very poor visual recall. Her parents were aware of her difficulties and would practise the spellings at home, getting her to write them out repeatedly until she could write them but most often she was in tears before this. This was creating friction and unhappiness at home and school. The class spelling list was taken from the National Literacy Strategy and was age-appropriate to the class. The problem was that in Year 5 the spellings were becoming increasingly complex and Jemma was falling further behind her peers, her self-esteem was suffering and she was starting to present with behaviour problems.

She came to me just before Christmas along with the class spelling list. It was essential to find out what Jemma knew, noting which common spelling rules she knew and the examples she could give me plus her knowledge of the alphabet and the sounds. She had a thorough knowledge of phonemes and a good knowledge of many of the rules but these were not assisting her in Year 5 when she was being presented with exceptions to the rules to learn and such a variety of words that it was almost impossible to build on previous learning. It was clear that tackling the spelling directly was only dealing with the observable outcome of poor visual processing. The priority was to improve her memory and visual recall as well as her understanding of how words are constructed. Practice started with memory games, particularly the 'challenge me' game and 'Kim's game'. Soon Jemma was remembering 23 items with little difficulty, and the task now was to apply this new-found confidence and skill to words. So we moved on to minimal pairs using some of the words from the spelling lists. We played them as pairs, we played them as finding words as quickly as possible, we moved this skill into finding particular words in books as quickly as possible and timing her. The parents were invited in to one teaching session to show them how to teach and practise spelling using games. They were amazed at how long she concentrated and how she willingly participated in spelling activities which had previously elicited tantrums.

REFLECTIVE TASK

Look at the spelling lists for Year 5 in the National Strategy.

Group these into lists of similar rules or visual patterns that you could use in a limited way with a child experiencing difficulties.

What prior knowledge is required to learn these words?

PRACTICAL TASK PRACTICAL TASK PRACTICAL TASK PRACTICAL TASK PRACTICAL TASK

Keep a tally of spelling strategies: phonics, look and say and analogy, for two days. Make sure you include as many strategies as possible.

How many activities that go on in classes are still paper based? Keep a tally for two days. Try to adapt 'dry paper-based tasks' to be games and bring motivation and multisensory teaching to bear on the learning process.

How much ICT was used? Try to use ICT to develop games based on popular TV programmes.

A SUMMARY OF **KEY POINTS**

> **Spelling is a complex task requiring core skills – check these core skills first before attempting to teach children more spellings.**

> **Spelling involves both phonic and visual abilities as well as a good understanding of how the English language works, i.e. knowledge of the rules. Make sure you have a good balance of these.**

> **Spelling needs over-learning with dyslexic children; you need to provide sufficient over-learning that is stimulating and motivating.**

> **You should aim to provide different ways for all children in the class to consolidate spelling so that the dyslexic children do not feel 'special' in any negative way.**

MOVING *ON* > > > > > > MOVING *ON* > > > > > > MOVING *ON*

Design one game to use with a child who experiences difficulty with phonics; keep it as open to variation as possible. Focus on initial consonants only. Try it out and evaluate it with a child. Redesign if necessary.

REFERENCES REFERENCES **REFERENCES** REFERENCES **REFERENCES** REFERENCES

Cox, B (1989) *English 5–16*. DfES. London: HMSO

DfES (2007) *Primary National Strategy*. London: DfES

Ehri, LC (2005) Reading processes, acquisition, and instructional implications, in Reid, G and Wearmouth, J (2005) *Dyslexia and literacy theory and practice.* Chichester: John Wiley and Sons

Giles, D and Terrell, C (1997) Visual sequential memory and spelling ability. *Educational Psychology,* 17 (3)

Goswami, U and Ziegler, J (2006) A developmental perspective on the neural code for written words. *Trends in Cognitive Sciences* 10 (4) 142–5

Hornsby, B (1995) *Overcoming dyslexia. A straightforward guide for families and teachers.* London: Vermillion

Montgomery, D (ed.) (2000) *Able underachievers.* London: Whurr Publishing

Ott, P (1997) *How to detect and manage dyslexia: a reference and resource manual.* Oxford: Heinemann

Pollock, J and Waller, E (2001) *Day-to-day dyslexia in the classroom.* Abingdon: RoutledgeFalmer.

Porter, L (2002) *Educating young children with special needs.* London: Paul Chapman Publishing

Pumfrey, P and Reason, R (1997) *Specific learning difficulties (dyslexia) challenges and responses.* Abingdon: Routledge

5
Teaching writing skills

Chapter objectives

By the end of this chapter you should be aware of:

- the main difficulties children experience in writing;
- the different aspects which go to make up the whole activity of writing;
- the main processes of writing in normal development;
- a variety of games and activities which will assist you in developing writing skills in dyslexic children;
- practical resources that will benefit children with writing difficulties.

This chapter addresses the following Professional Standards for QTS:

Q10, Q15, Q22, Q23, Q25(d).

Introduction

Writing is still considered one of the skills of an educated person in the Western world. Lack of ability to write marks a person as uneducated despite any other achievements. While there are iconic figures such as Richard Branson, Jackie Stewart and Susan George who have acquired celebrity status despite being dyslexic, there are far more people who are hindered by their lack of writing skills. The advent of word-processing has removed much of the tedium of writing for many people but there is still the need to be able to hand-write certain tasks. Applications for jobs may require a handwritten response, forms almost invariably need to be handwritten and there is always the 'on the spot' query waiting to highjack the unwary. Writing then is still of prime importance in our culture. This chapter will explore the difficulties experienced by dyslexic children and suggest ways of encouraging the development of good writing and the confidence to write. Ofsted (1999) noted that *greater attention must be given to the formal teaching of writing skills to these pupils*. The report goes on to note how the use of word-processing is of great advantage to pupils with specific learning difficulties; however, the danger of such pronouncements, where teachers are not sufficiently confident to use word-processing or where the curriculum mitigates against its use, is that 'formal' is interpreted as worksheets; this need not be so. Formal can be in the use of games and writing frames but does need to be structured to the needs of the children and it needs to be informed by knowledge of what the difficulties are.

Theoretical background

How important is writing really? Give a quick response to this. Don't think too much about it. Many people would say that in this day and age of technology, emailing, texting with its misspellings, correct grammatical writing is not too important.

BEELECLIAE IVZK

REFLECTIVE TASK

- List all examples of writing that you have experienced in the past five days. Separate them into personal writing, where you are the reader, and public, where someone else is the reader. Now separate them into formal and informal.

- Now answer the question: How important is writing? Do we still need to teach writing?

What is this thing called writing – product or process?

Writing is one of the most obvious aspects in which a dyslexic child may display difficulties. It is also generally the last of the literacy skills to be developed and is heavily influenced by speaking and listening and reading. Much of what is written at all stages of writing is crafted by what we read. The two are interrelated. My writing of this book is influenced by texts I have read, either accommodating writing styles or rejecting styles. In order to improve writing it is important first and foremost to provide the child with a guide of what writing looks like and what it can be about; you can achieve this by reading more to the children. Reading can also provide a starting point for their own writing by using a section of what has been read for adaptation by the child. Children will need to have been read to a lot, to have heard language a lot before they assimilate its forms ready for using them as a template for writing.

There are several skills involved in writing and children do not necessarily display difficulties in all of them. Spelling is a key area which was discussed in detail in the previous chapter. Other aspects of writing which may prove problematic are handwriting, layout, stamina, construction of writing, editing of writing and motivation to complete.

Development of writing

Development of writing rests on the following.

- Having something to say and an audience to whom it is addressed, i.e. a purpose.
- A model (or template) in the brain to follow.
- The ability to recreate known words (sight words).
- The ability to create words from known sounds (phonics).
- The ability to form letters correctly (orthography and handwriting).
- The ability to demarcate words.
- The ability to string words together sensibly to form sentences.
- The ability to string sentences together to form paragraphs.
- The ability to group sentences to form a cohesive text rather than a set of random thoughts.

The difficulties of the writing process may be plotted thus:

Thought /intention to convey meaning → pencil to paper, where to commence → directionality → decide on sentence → how to spell the first few words → writing the words – letter formation → remembering the sentence → spelling of rest of words → remembering what you intended to say → stamina → editing – this involves reading and memory, remembering what you intended to write.

Selikowitz (1998) has reduced these difficulties to the following list.

- *Motor planning difficulties.*
- *Visual perception difficulties.*
- *Pencil grip disorders.*
- *Visual memory deficit.*
- *Spatial planning deficit.*
- *Diminished rate or processing.* (p85).

Browne (2001) outlines the difficulties in a slightly different way as:

- *doesn't want to write;*
- *writes very little;*
- *never completes a piece of writing;*
- *poor spelling;*
- *disorganised and repetitive writing;*
- *poor punctuation;*
- *can't read what was written;*
- *poor handwriting.* (p207).

The following finer details add to this list of difficulties encountered in writing which are dyslexic-related.

- Poor handwriting, very angular with poor joins and formation from the wrong direction, poor spacing between words, with some words being squashed together while others have a huge space between them.
- Poor spelling, often bizarre, quite often reversals of letters or upside-down letters.
- Perseveration in spelling, where part of the spelling is repeated and repeated, for example *elelelephant* (where the 'el' part is repeated unnecessarily).
- Many crossings out, sometimes related to lack of confidence in spelling, sometimes relating to choice of word; however in most cases the final word will be the same as the original, and the final work will look very messy.
- Layout may be marked by work which starts at the left-hand margin but then systematically drifts in, not just to the centre line but often strays well over it to the right-hand margin where only a few words are written.
- Poor assessment of space available to write a word; long words will be started in a small space at the end of the line and will either be squashed or may swing back, or the text being written back to front.
- Mirror writing starting at the right-hand side and progressing left across the page is not common but is a marker to look out for.
- Writing which is confused and includes details which are not relevant or writing which is loosely connected but lacks cohesion.

Each can display singularly as the major difficulty but it may also affect other areas, for example poor handwriting may discourage a child from writing when in fact they have quite a bit to write about but they are embarrassed by the appearance of it.

The development of writing is closely related to the need and motivation to write. Speech is immediate and in response to a stimulus or need; often writing does not have this immediacy. As Whitehead (2004) notes, writing can be either a process or a product. It is the process that is being considered first and foremost here before the product.

Readiness to write

Early writing skills are developed in drawing. A child with immature drawings or who is unable to draw a relatively clear picture of a significant person will probably experience difficulty with writing. Remember also that a child will not write something they cannot articulate. Speaking and listening develop well before writing skills.

A child having difficulty holding a writing implement will not write easily as they will be concentrating on the physical aspect of holding the pencil/crayon.

It is important to be familiar with the 'normal' development of writing in order to be able to note when that development is not being followed. However, you still need to make allowances for individual differences and personal development.

Writing development

For most children their own name is one of the first words they learn to write, and many children achieve this before they enter school. Campbell (2001) outlines why this is so important to most children. Often these first attempts display evidence of a growing awareness of print and include virtuous errors. At this early stage children need to know and learn that letters are specific in their orientation. Unlike other objects around them in the world which maintain constancy whichever way they are rotated, letters and numbers must be written in a specific way. It is common for young children to write *b* for *d* or vice versa, however, with constant and sensitive tuition most children grow out of this by Key Stage 2. The child who perseveres with reversals is showing signs of a different development which is worth noting. Virtuous errors such as writing 'said' as 'siad' display a knowledge of the letters of the word but a lack of memory for their order. Again this is normal with most children up to Key Stage 2 but the child who continues in this way needs to be observed closely.

Most children in Key Stage 1 have difficulty in maintaining a straight line when writing, or in writing 'on the line'. Again, with careful and consistent support most children manage to perfect this by Key Stage 2.

This chapter is now going to examine specific aspects of writing and suggest practical ways to overcome difficulties.

Factors which can affect the presentation of writing

Poor posture is one of the most common reasons why children have poor handwriting. Before exploring any of the technical issues related to writing, you should check the following:

- Is the child sitting upright in their chair?
- Can the child put their feet on the floor in order to balance their weight?
- Is the table too high for the child?
- Does the child angle the page the correct way for their handedness?

There are easy ways of remediating these issues. A box placed under the child's feet can give them stability, a cushion or raised chair or lower table will solve the height of the chair-to-table aspect.

Paper should be angled 45° from their body line towards the non-writing hand. That is, a right-handed person should have their paper 45° towards their left-hand side so that the paper slants upwards to their mid-line. The opposite applies for a left-handed person. This is especially important for left-handed writers (which is common with dyslexic children) because if they have their paper in the same direction as right-handed children they cover their text as they are writing. When this happens children often develop a hooked pencil hold. The light should be over the non-writing shoulder in order not to cast a shadow on the writing.

Many children also benefit from a slanted surface. This can be achieved with the aid of a ring binder laid flat on its side with the larger spine edge away from the child, thus providing a slanting surface. Paper which is secured at the corners stops it from sliding around while the child writes.

Other practical suggestions are provided by Hall (2004, 2005), many of which can be used with other learning disabilities.

Handwriting
It is common practice in many schools to start children writing with very thick pencils. This makes the grip on such pencils for little hands quite difficult and, contrary to popular belief that fat pencils aid writing, there is a growing feeling that it does exactly the opposite. Imagine, if you can, trying to write with a pencil the size of a broom handle and you will appreciate the difficulty of writing with a fat pencil. This is where individualised learning really has to be seen to be practised. Some children will need a thick pencil, many will need a slimmer pencil, some will respond better to felt-tip or ballpoint as this is what they have been using at home. Pencil grips are a good idea to develop the correct position of fingers; however, this does not stop the death-like grip some children have on pencils. In order to combat this a short-term solution is to make a pencil grip out of modelling clay which squashes when gripped too much. The child should learn quickly to hold the pencil with a lighter grip.

Hot, sticky hands are another problem and cause the child's fingers to slide down the pencil. Again a pencil grip can provide an answer but a cheaper option is to wind either an elastic band or a piece of sticky tape around the base of the pencil, so preventing the fingers from sliding.

For older children Hornsby (1995) recommends the use of fountain pens as this forces the correct position for the pen to work. Not many schools use fountain pens these days but a chisel-tipped marker can be as good as these and will only work in a certain position.

It is important to start handwriting formation practice as soon as possible. This should not be a class exercise as happens in many schools. For this to be effective you need to sit with a group of children and watch how they form their letters and correct both their pencil grip and the formation of their letters before they develop a hold or formation which later hinders them. Handwriting practice should not be tedious, it should be fun. You can devise your own practice sheets or purchase ready-prepared ones. Each sheet should practise the movement required for a particular letter and then apply that movement to the letter. Practice of this sort should happen at least twice daily with a particular group of children for it to be effective.

Practise the letter m
Trace over the fence and rail track.
Draw another large caterpillar on the path.

Example of practice sheet for handwriting suitable for Key Stage 1.

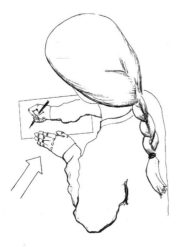

Pressure or excess pressure is a difficulty with dyslexic children. A technique to relieve this pressure in the writing hand is to ask them to press the other hand on the table while they write.

This has to be developed early on before excess pressure becomes a constant way of writing. Once it becomes a common practice the child needs to be taught to recognise the pressure and the effect it has on the tendons and muscles in the wrist and hand. At this point they need to be taught relaxation exercises to relieve the effects. Exercises such as balling the hand into a fist then opening the hand and flexing the fingers helps, as does imaginary piano playing or squeezing and releasing a soft ball.

Letter formation can be assisted by the use of double-lined paper. This will plot where the top of the lower case letters should sit and where the capitals should reach to.

In the early stages a green dot to show the start of a particular letter then an orange arrow to show the course of the letter with a red dot to show the finish position helps many children to develop the correct formation of letters. If left to their own devices many children will start their letters on the line in an attempt to make sure their writing does 'sit on the line'. This works for some letters but not for the majority of script letters which should be formed from above the line. This is one reason why joined writing has become so prominent. Joined writing automatically ensures the correct formation of letters, dispenses with word demarcation problems and often teaches automatic spelling. I cannot commend joined writing (of whichever style) to you too strongly.

PRACTICAL TASK PRACTICAL TASK **PRACTICAL TASK** PRACTICAL TASK **PRACTICAL TASK**

Select a piece of writing to copy. Copy this using print script and concentrate on how you form your letters. Now copy the same text using joined writing. What were the differences between the two in terms of where you started your letters? How much did you have to think about the script version? Which aspects did you think about?

Slant and layout

One of the difficulties many dyslexic children have is keeping their writing in a straight line and keeping the slant of their writing consistent. This is often because their paper is poorly positioned (see above). It can also be because they have not had enough practice at writing. This is a real problem and is related to motivation and stamina. As Browne (2001) opines:

> For less successful writers there is often little enthusiasm for the process. Writing is slow and painful and as a result they do less writing than their more successful peers. Because they engage less in the process, they receive less practice, less help and less positive feedback and begin to think of themselves as unable to write. This can result in unwillingness to write. (p201)

There are two aspects to this difficulty: the need or motivation to write and the actual act of writing and keeping the lettering straight and well rounded. While most primary classrooms would develop the two in harmony, for dyslexic children it may be better to revert to the traditional practice of handwriting practice being separate. However, it is still important to imbue this activity with some purpose. A display of poetry (for handwriting practice as well as developing language skills) is a suitable means of promoting good handwriting. Time should be allowed for handwriting and breaking the task into small chunks is helpful as dyslexic pupils will be slow in writing and need regular breaks. To start with, the use of squared paper can be useful in keeping the slant and size of letters in the right direction.

Once the writing is relatively regular, return to normal paper. If handwriting is very poor, teachers should consider the use of laptops and other assistive technology. Some severely dyslexic pupils will display unreadable handwriting which even when improved is still very untidy and poorly presented. You could not let such pupils go into adult life with this type of handwriting.

Compositional aspects

Many children, even non-dyslexic children, are often heard to say *I don't know what to write*. This can be for several reasons.

- You are asking them to undertake a task for which they do not have a mental template (form or genre of writing).
- You are asking them to write about something they have no experience of (for example, what it is like to be an orphan).
- You are asking them to write about something they find boring or can see no purpose in.
- You are asking them to record the topic in a tedious fashion or one which suits you but not their own learning style.
- You have presented them with too large an expanse of paper to write on and have frightened them off.

It is alarming that many texts ignore this aspect of writing and focus on spelling and handwriting only as worthy of attention. The following texts focus on spelling and handwriting but do not mention composition of the written word at all: Ott (1997), Selikowitz (1998), Pollock and Waller (2001), Wray and Medwell (2008). All of these are texts, which provide information and instruction on how to teach spelling and handwriting – ignore the compositional aspect. Indeed it seems that only non-fiction writing is worth any mention at all; this can be found in Wray (2006) where writing frames and modelled writing are suggested as ways of tutoring children in this genre of writing. It would appear that other forms of writing are expected to be picked up by osmosis.

Generating and capturing ideas for writing

The importance of fun and creativity cannot be overemphasised with dyslexic children, particularly older children. Older children will have already learnt to fail and failed at the usual sorts of activities offered in the mainstream classroom. To offer them the same again is inviting repeated failure. You need to think laterally and devise activities which will engage their interest, allow them to display what they can do and have a purpose to them. Much good writing rests on other activities such as drama, art and music, watching a video, talking about an event, planning an event, planning and writing newspaper articles for a class paper, planning and writing booklets as a classroom resource, etc. All of these activities can lead to writing which has a purpose and a real audience. They may also use incidental writing such as writing prompt cards in drama. These incidental activities provide children with short bursts of writing for a real purpose and provide them with practice as well.

Games which require the child to write a note or make a note of a detail are good ways to get reluctant writers to write. You can either make your own game or use a commercially based one. Games such as murder mystery activities or solving a puzzle provide fun activities, where they have to write down information as it comes to light, and are good for Key Stage 2 children. You could vary the 'I went to market and bought' to include writing the list as it goes along, with the aim of seeing who can write the longest list and still read it at the end.

Challenges such as collecting the most words beginning with a certain letter also prompt children to write while having fun.

Suggestions of ways to stimulate writing can be found in Evans's excellent book *The writing classroom aspects of writing and the primary age child 3–11* (2001). Writing in any form may not take place until the third or fourth lesson and you need to be sure of how you can justify these activities which lead up to the moment of writing. These activities not only give a context to writing but help to engage the child and relax them. You also have to rotate the activities and intersperse the writing at different points in order to keep the children 'on their toes'.

You are almost hoodwinking the child into not expecting a writing task, quite the converse of what happens in many classrooms where if a book is read you may be able to hear children saying *Are we going to have to write about this afterwards?* Svantesson (1998) declares *Creativity is stimulated when we move the balance a little towards chaos and disorder. That is an explanation of why most people are creative when they have fun or are relaxed* (p19).

The moment of writing properly

Having been provided with a stimulus, the moment of writing is a frightening one for many dyslexic children. You need to provide support and reassurance for them that they can do the task. This may involve providing some key words for them as most older dyslexic children are extremely concerned about their spelling. It may involve using concept maps and other ways of recording thoughts as suggested by Svantesson (1998). Free concept mapping software can be downloaded from www.thebrain.com/#-47 and can provide a structure for many children, or the child may find their own way of recording ideas however disorganised it seems to you.

However, you do not need complicated programs to facilitate this sort of 'disorganised thinking'. Different ways of recording thoughts may not just be linear, some of the following, available from Windows, can be used.

This form is useful for children who do not know what the central idea is or where to start with a central idea. They only know their thoughts fit together somehow. If they cut the jigsaw up afterwards they can reorganise the jigsaw even if it doesn't fit together again.

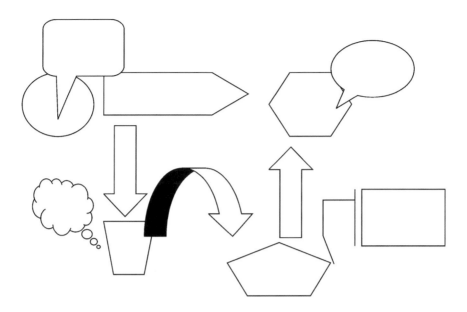

This complicated form of flowchart has no start or finish, it just allows the child to enter information and then to organise it. There is no compunction to complete all of the sections, and more sections can be added as needed.

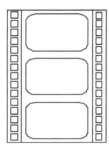

Although this is a linear representation, many children do respond well to the thought of a film script idea. Again, parts of the film can be cut up and re-ordered if necessary.

More ideas generated by Tony Buzan are available at www.creativethinkingwith.com/Tony-Buzan.html

Getting organised

Once ideas are recorded, the next step is to organise them into something sensible. The use of a writing frame where the edge of the writing area is demarcated and a limited number of lines presented is useful in encouraging children to start writing. The visual impact of this limited space is supportive to children who fear they cannot write a lot or have difficulties knowing where to start on the page.

For very hesitant writers it may be necessary to scribe for some of the text (Browne, 2001). It is best if you allow the child to write something themselves and for you to alternate between them writing and you writing. In this way you can encourage them to write more without forcing them to write more than they feel comfortable with. Another strategy is to keep asking questions in written form for them to answer; this keeps them writing and at the end you can praise them for the amount they have written.

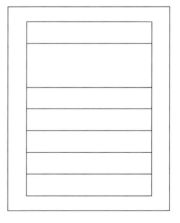

Example of a writing frame

Activities to get children writing

Written work should be for a real audience as much as possible. The audience can be other children in the same class, for example when booklets are made as a resource for the class, it may be other children in other classes when stories have been written for them. The audience may be outside, as in parents reading newsletters, or it may be themselves or younger children. It is challenging for you to find these audiences but the result is well worth the effort. It is equally important that you educate the parents about this process and the fact that the children are becoming writers (authors) and need praise and encouragement.

A technique in story writing is for each child in a small group to write the start of a story, the passage is then passed to the next child who reads the start and continues the story for a paragraph. The story is then passed to the next child. Depending on whether this is a well-known story or a made-up creative story and the age of the children you may need to give quite explicit instructions on what you want in each section, such as *You are to describe the next place you see, this place is happy place and I want you to describe it as best you can*. In this way a group activity is shared among all children in the group, it involves reading and writing and the group takes responsibility for it and receives the praise for it as well as individual children feeling proud of their contribution. They should also have the chance to illustrate it.

Too often illustration is seen as a time-filler after the real work has been done. However, if you think of the drafting process which usually involves written language to clarify thoughts, is there any reason why drawings should not be used to help and stimulate thoughts about a story? This is in fact the way many author–illustrators work, the drawings prompting the thoughts. It is well worth attempting this sometimes rather than the other way around. The fear here is that you will have at least one, maybe two lessons with nothing more than drawings to show for the time. If, at the end of the three or four lessons, you then have a well-constructed and imaginative written piece, was the time spent drafting not well worth it?

Poetry is an ideal genre to coax children into reading and writing. The pattern of rhyming verse helps struggling readers and poems usually are written in stanzas which can be read in short energy bursts. Deleting some of the rhyming words can provide an interesting activity for many children with dyslexia. This is not a new activity but one which is often overlooked with dyslexic children. They can supply the missing word. When this is done in a group, each individual poem may be different while still following a theme. The new version can be displayed along with the original version.

The use of the writing frame is open to adaptation. For very hesitant writers you can include only a few lines within a very narrowly demarcated area. As the child progresses you can widen the area and introduce more lines to the frame.

The process of editing

It is a good idea when a child starts writing on plain paper or the normal A4 paper to write on alternate lines and only on one side of the paper. This allows for corrections and additions to be made to the text between the written lines and it also allows for the writer to cut up the text and move pieces around, on the table, without having to rewrite it. It may seem like a waste of paper but the impact of this tactile editing can have tremendous results. It is important not to expect the work to be in the correct order to start with. As adult writers, when we write we very often undertake several drafts before we are happy with something:

why should children be any different? Furthermore, Svantesson (1998) supports the proposition that the brain does not work in a linear way but remembers key words.

Punctuation

Punctuation is a device to show readers how to read a text, where to pause, where to put extra emphasis. It is not a device for writers; the writer knows where to stop and where to put an inflection; however, it is in writing that punctuation is used to inform the reader. How do we get over this hurdle? Simply ask the writer, or another child, to read the work onto an audio recorder. This captures the text as it is and indicates to the writer where punctuation is needed. The writer can also go back to the text time and again, rewinding the recorder to correct the writing. This stage will come after the child has finished composing their writing.

CASE STUDY

Jack was quite a loquacious child in Year 2, always able to speak about different subjects at length, but he reverted to avoidance tactics when presented with any written work. He was very knowledgeable about science and enjoyed science where he could either complete work in a group or just fill in forms/worksheets. He was extremely good at art and very musical. These were his strengths but they were not really valued in a school which prided itself on its place in the league tables. One member of staff said *We are not really an arty school, or a musical one.* Any written work that was completed by Jack was unreadable and/or unfinished. He became truculent at writing times and did everything in his power to avoid writing, including going to the toilet, pushing items onto the floor so that he could retrieve them, finding his shoelace undone and needing to tie it up. By the time he had returned to the task he had 'forgotten' what he had to do. It was necessary to be more devious than Jack in order to engage him.

He was amazed that on our first proper lesson we didn't actually do any writing at all but just talked about what writing could be used for, why we write, and I read him a story from a picture book. The look on his face at the pictures in *Outside over there* by Maurice Sendak was pure enchantment. I managed to persuade the classroom teacher to mirror work in the classroom around this text and an arbour was made in art with some groups which Jack contributed to. Ice was studied in science – again engaging Jack. For the next lesson I had brought a selection of music from which Jack could choose the piece he thought most appropriate to go with a section of the book. We also discussed how he had helped make the arbour and this conversation was tape-recorded. Jack was gradually being drawn into the topic of the book and becoming relaxed and losing his apprehension about our lessons.

In the main class not all of the groups had made their arbour or contributed to the main arbour being built in the classroom and the lowest-ability reading group had been left until last for a purpose. In our writing sessions it was explained to Jack that the groups left needed some help and instruction with their arbours and it would be helpful if he wrote some instructions on how to make the arbour. His first reaction was as predicted: *I can't write.* Then he used logic *Why can't I just tell them?* Then *I've forgotten how I made it.*

The tape-recording of his conversation was brought out and we (he, with a bit of persuasion) decided that the writing would go on cards because a whole sheet might be too much for the remaining groups to read. So we listened to how he constructed his arbour and again talked a lot about what was needed first and this was written on a

---

card with a lot of help and encouragement and some modelling of good writing so that it could be read. The tape was played again and the next instruction was written on the second card, then the third. It was decided at this point that he had written enough to get the next group started. (His writing was also starting to deteriorate rapidly at this point.)

The following week he came bouncing into class to start his writing, which by now he had miraculously remembered how to do because the remaining groups were nagging him for the instructions on how to complete their arbours. With a bit of help and some alternate scribing and provision of key words, he completed the task in that lesson. In other lessons we found an outlet in order to practise his handwriting which needed attention but at least we had overcome his reluctance to write – for now.

He then wanted to word-process his work so that it looked neater. This presented another problem – the case study in the ICT chapter, Chapter 8.

REFLECTIVE TASK
REFLECTIVE TASK

Watch a writing activity/lesson with a group of struggling writers or just the ordinary class.

Have ready a score sheet sectioned into spelling, handwriting, organisation and composition. Observe and keep a tally for each occasion that the teacher makes a comment about each of these categories. Which one has the highest score? What implicit message is being given about writing?

Consider how you would move these children on in composition and how you would also attend to their spelling and handwriting.

A SUMMARY OF **KEY POINTS**

> Make sure that other factors such as seating, desk height and paper orientation are correct.
> Make sure you are clear in your own mind which aspects of writing you are addressing at any one time; be familiar with the different aspects of writing yourself.
> Make writing purposeful and fun.
> Use formats that assist rather than hinder the pupil.
> Use ideas mapping or other techniques to record the thought processes at the start.
> Break writing tasks up into manageable chunks.
> Liaise with parents who can supervise writing at home and provide more practice for their child.
> Liaise with your SENCo.

MOVING *ON* > > > > > > MOVING *ON* > > > > > > MOVING *ON*

Having realised that for struggling writers you need to engage and be creative, you need to provide constant support, which may be difficult in many classrooms. You now need to consider your classroom organisation in order to facilitate this support. If this means moving some of the literacy activities to the afternoon to allow different groupings and time, then this must be considered. If it means your teaching assistant is only available at certain times to support these children or that the teaching assistant needs to go on a course to support the children, then this is your goal. The important issue is that you get these children writing and not in an unwilling way! This will not stick with them. Learning has to be memorable.

REFERENCES REFERENCES **REFERENCES** REFERENCES **REFERENCES** REFERENCES

Browne, A (2001) *Developing language and literacy 3–8.*, London: Paul Chapman Publishing

Campbell, R (2001) 'That's how I used to write my name when I was little', under-fives exploring writing, in Evans, J *The writing classroom. Aspects of writing and the primary child 3–11.* London: David Fulton

Evans, J (ed.) (2001) *The writing classroom. Aspects of writing and the primary child 3–11.* London: David Fulton

Hall, W (2004) Inclusion: special needs, in Bold, C (ed.) *Supporting learning and teaching.* London: David Fulton

Hall, W (2005) Making the most of the teaching assistant for special educational needs, in Campbell, A and Fairbairn, G (eds) *Working with support in the classroom.* London: Paul Chapman Publishing

Hornsby, B (1995) *Overcoming dyslexia. A straightforward guide for families and teachers.* London: Vermillion

Montgomery, D (ed.) (2000) *Able underachievers.* London: Whurr Publishing

Ofsted (1999) *Pupils with specific learning difficulties in mainstream schools.* London: HMSO

Ott, P (1997) *How to detect and manage dyslexia.* Oxford: Heinemann.

Pollock, J and Waller, E (2001) *Day-to-day dyslexia in the classroom.* Abingon: RoutledgeFalmer

Porter, L (2002) *Educating young children with special needs.* London: Paul Chapman Publishing

Selikowitz, M (1998) *Dyslexia and other learning difficulties: the facts.* Oxford: Oxford University Press

Svantesson, I (1998) *Learning maps and memory skills.* London: Kogan Page

Whitehead, M (2004) *Language and literacy in the early years.* London: Sage

Wray, D (2006) *Teaching literacy across the primary curriculum.* Exeter: Learning Matters

Wray, D and Medwell, J (2008) *Extending knowledge in practice. Primary English.* Exeter: Learning Matters

Useful websites

The brain visual information management www.thebrain.com/#-47

Creative thinking with Tony Buzan www.creativethinkingwith.com/Tony-Buzan.html

6
Teaching reading: games and activities

Chapter objectives

By the end of this chapter you should be aware of:

- **the skills necessary to teach reading and the different ways children will learn many aspects of reading;**
- **the difficulties many dyslexic children encounter in trying to learn our complicated language;**
- **a variety of games and activities which will enhance the teaching and learning of core skills to improve children's ability to read.**

This chapter addresses the following Professional Standards for QTS:

Q10, Q15, Q22, Q23, Q25(a), (b), (d).

Introduction

When the word 'dyslexia' is mentioned, most people assume reading is affected. This is so in most cases, however, the way in which reading is affected and the extent to which it is affected may differ according to the subtype of dyslexia a person experiences. This chapter outlines the different types of dyslexia and how reading may or may not be affected and provides some strategies for addressing the issues raised.

Theoretical background

Reading is one of the aspects of literacy that dyslexic children have difficulty with, second only to spelling for many children. Indeed these two aspects of literacy are inextricably linked. As Ehri (1997) states, spelling is not just a process but a product to be read. Reading involves basic concepts such as knowing that print carries meaning; in English the written text must be read left to right in most instances, the concept of letter, word and sentence boundaries. Punctuation has an important role to play in reading; poor readers often ignore this and read without pausing or observing punctuation which might provide inflection to certain words. Even when these concepts are understood and embedded, the reader must recognise the word as a unit of meaning and 'decode' it, they must also then assimilate a group of words to form a sentence with a larger meaning than just the word provides. Indeed it is often the sentence which provides the exact meaning to the decoding of individual words. A child may be able to read the words 'fly' or 'dress' but will be unsure of their meaning until they are placed in a sentence which will denote either of these words as either a noun or a verb. *The fly was on the food* creates a totally different concept, mental image and understanding of the word 'fly' from the sentence *We can fly to France. The dress needed to be washed* provides a different mental image from *We had to dress quickly*.

Furthermore, there are homographs, which look the same but are pronounced differently according to the context. *Live* and *live*, *present* and *present* are pronounced differently depending on their meaning; the difficulty is that the reader does not know how to say the word until the meaning is understood and often the meaning is obscured by mispronouncing the word in the first place, causing a block for dyslexic children. They need to be able to process both sounds mentally and decide on the correct one.

From this we can see that reading operates at several levels: there is the level where a reader can recognise or sound out a word but does not know what it means or may not even pronounce it properly; there is the level where they can say the word and give meaning to it but are unsure of the exact meaning; and there is the level where the words can be said, an informed choice made about the reading of the word and the exact meaning is understood. These different levels are referred to as:

- surface structure – the words as we see them;
- deep structure – the meaning the author wants to create by the use of the words.

After this there is the need to remember what has been read in order to comprehend the whole text whether that is at paragraph level or chapter level. Memory plays a key part in the ability to read. Pollock and Waller (2001) note that even when decoding skills are developed, there are often residual difficulties with meaning.

Moreover, there is not just one way to teach reading but there are many different ways to introduce and teach the skills necessary to become a successful reader in terms of methods and resources. No one method or resource will suit all children. As long ago as 1967 Plowden wrote:

> As to the systematic teaching that follows this introduction to reading and writing, the most successful infant teachers have refused to follow the wind of fashion and to commit themselves to any one method. They choose methods and books to fit the age, interest and ability of individual pupils. (Para 584)

The independent review of early reading (Rose, 2004), which has guided the most recent government initiatives on reading, stating that phonics is the best way to teach reading, has largely ignored the needs of dyslexic children. Indeed, Sir Jim Rose at a TDA conference in London on 7 October 2008 stated that he had not taken full account of the difficulties of dyslexic children, or researched this area sufficiently when he wrote the review. He acknowledged *I rather walked into a hornets' nest on that one*. He is now participating in a review of provision for children with dyslexia as part of the response to the 'No to Failure' project. (Dyslexia Contact, 2008)

Connors, an assistant professor at the Florida Centre for Reading Research, stated as recently as 2007 in a publication called *No One Strategy Is Best For Teaching Reading:*

> [L]ots of individualized instruction, combined with the use of diagnostic tools that help teachers match each child with the amounts and types of reading instruction that are most effective for him or her, is vastly preferable to the standard 'one size fits all' approach to reading education that is prevalent.

She further states *Instead of viewing the class as an organism, we're trying to get teachers to view the students as individuals.*

While Rose (2004) does state that phonics should be *securely embedded within a broad and language rich curriculum,* Wyse and Styles (2007) state that the advocacy of synthetic phonics contradicts this aim.

This rationale is the basis for constructing suitable teaching materials for children with dyslexia. It could even be argued that this should be the basis for teaching all children. Good teaching for dyslexic children is good teaching for all children. However, the present government has different views and has put forward the phonic method as being best. This needs intelligent reflection on the part of teachers teaching dyslexic children.

The difficulties dyslexic children have with the process of reading include:

- not recognising the sounds of letters;
- not being able to sequence the sounds in a word;
- forgetting the sequence and not being able to make a recognisable word;
- not recognising the visual sequence of letters and not remembering sight words;
- being able to say words but not being able to remember them in a sentence and thus not being able to extract meaning;
- not being able to generalise fonts, so not recognising the same grapheme in different fonts;
- mispronouncing words so they are not recognisable as a word stored in the lexicon;
- not being able to recognise or assign meaning to punctuation which helps with meaning and intonation when reading aloud.

Aside from these factors which directly hinder the progress of reading, there are secondary factors, even when decoding is relatively efficient, such as lack of stamina in reading, becoming easily tired, losing one's place when reading, missing a line or re-reading the same line without realising it, forgetting what has been read and lack of engagement with reading.

Many dyslexic children will also exhibit signs of scotopic sensitivity syndrome, which can cause headaches, eye strain and visual resolution difficulties. Moving print is a very common complaint when a child has both dyslexia and scotopic sensitivity syndrome. The print needs to be stabilised before remedial reading tuition is likely to be successful. Class teachers are advised to refer children complaining of headaches, colours on the page, flashing white or moving print to an educational psychologist for assessment for both scotopic sensitivity syndrome and dyslexia.

Phonics versus look and say

There are several ways of decoding or working out the surface structure of words. The present government promotes the use of phonics as the primary method of decoding words. Claims are made that children who learn synthetic phonics early on make greater gains than by any other method. Transfer to visual word recognition comes later in their development but phonics provides them with a means of decoding unfamiliar words that they have never encountered before. There are, though, several ways of splitting up words even within phonics: through phonemes, through onset and rime and through syllable division (Goswami and Bryant, 1990). All of these methods should be included in a programme for teaching dyslexic children. However, while it is widely accepted that for many dyslexic children a lack of phonological knowledge and understanding is the basis for their difficulties and they benefit from and need systematic tuition in this, there is equally a group of children with dyslexia who have extreme difficulty with phonics and who despite tuition still fail to thrive with this method. Teaching them by this method is not only unlikely to meet with success as this is their core deficit but is also likely to lead to frustration and feelings of failure. These children rely on visual memory for both reading and spelling from an early age, often only gaining a very sketchy grasp of phonics. That is not to say that as a teacher you should give up on them though, but that you have to employ different methods of teaching them so that they are not aware that they are being taught systematic phonics.

The second group of children with dyslexia have difficulty with visual sequences and usually have some success with phonology and may well succeed with this method but may then meet difficulty making the transition to word recognition and become totally dependent on phonics to decode words even as a mature reader. This then slows their reading development and makes fluent reading difficult.

The third, mixed, group have difficulty with both phonics and visual strategy and also needs consideration because they will experience difficulty at both these points in learning to read but in varying degrees. They will encounter some difficulty with early phonics but also some difficulty with the transition to whole-word reading.

The ultimate aim in reading is to make this transition to whole-word reading as the most immediate access to our lexicon. It is this immediate recall of words which allows us to read a sentence quickly and to attach an understanding to the group of words without having to decode and then remember each word individually.

Many dyslexic children experience difficulty at the early word-recognition stage either because they cannot attach sounds to letters and build up words, their attempts produce something totally unlike the word in front of them, or because they have poor visual recall and cannot recognise words even when only just read on the same page.

It is these skills of phonics and look and say which are at the core for early reading skills. It is essential that an informative diagnostic assessment is undertaken in order to devise a suitable teaching plan with relevant resources for dyslexic children. It should not be assumed that all dyslexic children have difficulty with reading or even the same difficulty with reading. Dyslexic children are as different from each other in their skills as there are different children in the group, i.e. each one is individual. The teaching programme should aim to remediate any deficits and also use the strengths of the child. Depending on the age of the child, they may already have well-developed coping strategies and have gaps which need addressing rather than a programme that attempts to teach them from a basic level.

It must never be forgotten, whatever the stage of tuition, that reading is essentially about extracting meaning. Even when we are focused on teaching decoding skills we should include activities which remind the child that reading is also about the whole text and meaning. It is meaning which makes the process of decoding worthwhile. A creative teacher can incorporate activities which combine both word recognition and meaning by substituting similar words with a different meaning so that the child not only has to look at the structure of the word but pay attention to the context of the word. The teacher may want to assume the greater responsibility for reading the sentence while the child is required to decode the individual word to select to make sense. Unfortunately the deficit in working memory hinders children in the process of extracting meaning. By the time the word has been decoded they may well have forgotten the context of the word. The same deficit makes 'sounding out' words difficult for the same reason; by the time each letter has been decoded and then sequenced the child may well have forgotten what the first few phonemes were. Sequencing itself poses problems for dyslexic children because of this short-term memory and working memory deficit.

Using games

The purpose of games is to increase motivation and engagement. This is more likely to happen through games than memorising words or analysing sounds to form words. It is likely too that dyslexic children may well have already started to fail by the usual methods of synthetic phonics or memorisation of word lists by the time they enter Year 1. They may well already view reading as 'hard work' and something they cannot do. Engaging in games, however, takes away the 'work' aspect of the activity and as Petty (2004) states: *Play can produce intense involvement and quality of concentration no other teaching method can match* (p234).

You should also use the widest possible resource bank and not just rely on the reading books provided in school. Indeed many of these books will already have associations of failure attached to them. Some of the most powerful reading tools are the environmental print around children, or their own culture such as comics, cartoon subtitles, etc., and their own writing. Poetry should not be ignored for its powerful ability to assist in reading using the predictability of rhyme. Goswami (1999) and Bryant et al. (1989) in their research support the use of rhyme in using onset and rime while acknowledging other phonic methods. Limericks, poems and jingles increase the ability to predict what might come next when children are familiar with rhyme. It is quite easy to select and construct texts which include the vocabulary from the Primary National Strategy or reading schemes as well as construct texts which assist in prediction if you have the willingness and ingenuity to do this. It is not a science and there is no great secret to it. However, it does take time to select and make your own resources. Joke books have proved to be successful with Key Stage 2 children who lack motivation to read the usual reading books provided in school. It is also essential to read accurately to gain the full impact of jokes. The laughter of a joke well delivered is enough to motivate many reluctant readers.

You will find that some of the games suggested here can be adapted to teach spelling and vice versa as spelling and reading are linked activities. Children generally learn to spell words they can read, and practice in spelling reinforces the ability to read the words. It is suggested that you integrate spelling and reading activities. The principles of multisensory techniques should also be evident so that children not only see and say letters and words but are encouraged to feel the shape of them on paper, in sand, in the air, etc. Goswami and Ziegler (2006) assert that phonology and orthography are intimately connected from the beginning of reading, therefore incorporating writing into reading aids the multisensory nature of reading.

Summary of the difficulties experienced by dyslexic children in learning to read

- Lack of knowledge of phoneme/grapheme correspondence.
- Limited concept formation; thinking sounds only refer to lowercase letters and names refer to uppercase.
- Difficulty with sequencing sounds to form a word.
- Difficulty in remembering sight words even when met before.

- Difficulty in remembering words just read in order to find meaning in a sentence.
- Difficulty in remembering previous sentences to find meaning in a paragraph.
- Slow and laborious reading due to decoding difficulties.
- Not remembering what has been read.
- Loss of place because of tiredness or concentration fatigue.
- Tiredness.
- Lack of interest.

The games and activities that follow are designed to develop different aspects of reading at various levels of development. Early phonics and look and say games are used in the early stages.

Once a child has developed the ability to recognise and remember words, they then need to develop the ability to extract meaning from sequences of words, to listen to what they are reading rather than to just decode a series of words. Context-reliant games are suggested for developing readers and text puzzles are suggested for more advanced readers. The later games are designed to develop this ability to listen to and pay attention to meaning.

Before moving on to the games, it is important to realise how we read and in what circumstances.

REFLECTIVE TASK
BEEFECLIAE 1V2K

Think of the different genres of reading you or your children engage in.

When do you need to read carefully for exact information?

When will a quick scan and general information be sufficient?

When do you resort to phonics?

How do you know when you have misread something? What do you then do?

Using games to develop reading skills

Principles for playing games
- Build on what children already know.
- Teach, practise and play with the vocabulary that is being taught through spelling.
- Introduce new vocabulary in a logical and cumulative way.
- Use multisensory techniques as much as possible to reinforce your main mode of teaching.
- Reinforce the underlying skills of visual and oral memory through games even when not directly related to the vocabulary being taught.
- Make sure some activities always focus on meaning, not just decoding.
- Use audio recorders to aid self-reflection and improvement.
- Use real texts as much as possible.
- Make sure you reinforce skills and tuition in other contexts and lessons to provide practice for over-learning.

Hints for using reading activities
- Children with dyslexia may also be dyspraxic, experiencing manipulation difficulties. Wind rubber bands around the edge of playing cards in order to give extra grip.

- Some children may need matt lamination to minimise glare. If you cannot get matt, you could spray your cards with hairspray – when this dries it leaves a matt finish.
- Use a minimum of 14-point bold text, preferably dark brown or blue in colour on cream-coloured card. This addresses the needs of both dyslexic children and children with scotopic sensitivity Syndrome which is often co-morbid with dyslexia. Comic sans (this font) is a font which is easily read with the traditional letter a and few curves, descenders and ascenders to confuse the eye. Most other fonts use letters with overly flourished letters such as the letters *g* and *a* which are hard for many dyslexic readers to recognise. The letter *y* is not formed in the way that handwriting is taught.
- Do not photocopy and enlarge real texts as this enlarges spaces as well as font. If necessary, retype the text and reproduce, copying selected pictures to accompany the text. Always accredit the text source.

The first few games will focus on the core skills.

Phonics games

The ability to read with phonics involves several sub-skills. These include the ability to:

- hear discrete sounds or phonemes;
- match the sound (phoneme) to a letter (grapheme);
- replicate these sounds and to sequence them in a remembered pattern;
- reconstruct a word from its constituent phonemes into a recognisable word;
- recognise words by analogy and to 'hear' the pattern in words;
- combine several patterns that have been learnt such as combining digraphs into a whole word;
- know the different sound patterns possible from any combination of letters such as 'ough' which can produce at least five different units of sound.

In the early stages of phonics it is essential that the child recognises the letters of the alphabet and knows the corresponding phonemes both for lower and uppercase letters. It is surprising how many children think the phonemes only relate to lowercase letters and letter names relate to the uppercase or capital letters. Children need to know both the phonemes and the letter names. Letter names are particularly relevant when reading medial vowels in words, as children quickly recognise that some medial vowels say their own name.

You will need several sets of resources in the early stages of checking grapheme-to-phoneme recognition including an alphabet card and individual letter cards. Many of the activities for teaching spelling using phonics can be used in the early stages of reading, such as the phonic bingo game.

The following activities will develop the ability to hear sounds and to think about sounds. They provide practice and repeated opportunities to think about sounds while the child is playing and having fun.

Game 1: Alphabet arc challenge

Aim: to support the ability to match sounds to letters
Resources required: an alphabet such as wooden letters or plastic letters, a card with the alphabet written on for the child to undertake a self-check.

How to play
Easy version

Ask the child to place the alphabet in the correct order, in the shape of a rainbow arc, and then to say the letters. When they are happy with the result they can check accuracy against their alphabet card. Prompt them to check not only for order but for reversals, etc. Reversing j, L, b and d are very common. Placing G and J interchangeably is also an easy mistake at this stage and can cause persistent difficulties.

Now ask the child to turn away while you move or remove some of the letters which the child has to identify have been changed.

To finish this activity you should ask the child to return the letters to the storage bag in the order in which you say the phonemes/letter names. When there are only four letters left ask the child what they are.

Harder versions
Time the child in placing the arc out and then in replacing it back in the bag.

Place the arc out yourself and place certain letters in the wrong position, then ask the child to find them and correct the order.

Support this game by using the phonic bingo game to reinforce the learning of individual letter sound and name.

Game 2: Air writing on the back
Aim: to support the ability to identify letter shapes and assign a sound

Resources required: none

How to play
Turn the child around so that they are facing away from you. Tell them to close their eyes and imagine a big board in front of them. They are going to 'see' and imagine the letter you are going to draw on their back.

Draw a letter with your finger on their back and describe the shape of it as you write it. For example, the letter c would be *start at the top of the letter, now curl it around so that it is nice and round, sit it on the line, but you are not making a complete circle*. The letter h would be *start up in the air at the top of the letter now come down in a straight line to the bottom of the letter, now take your finger half way up again and jump a bump, over and back down again*.

Now get the child to repeat this pattern with their finger in the air (you could use a sand tray or wipe-clean board if you wish). When they have correctly drawn the letter, ask them what the letter sound is and if they know the name. An extension activity to this is to ask for a word that starts in with this sound.

Game 3: Phoneme snap and bingo
Aim: to support the ability to hear sounds
The ability to match sounds to graphemes is crucial in phonics. This game supports both the reading of words using synthetic phonics and the ability to spell using analytic phonics.

Resources required: a set of cards with graphemes or digraphs written on them, baseboards.

How to play
Start with snap. Make sure that the child has a good grounding of knowing the phonemes through the use of the arc first. Deal the cards. Play snap by each player placing a card on the pile. The snap occurs when two cards with the same phoneme are placed down, so for example a child could snap s and then c because they can both say the phoneme *ssss* similarly s and sh could be snapped because they can both say *sh*. This concentrates the child on the many combinations of phonemes that are possible and not the visual image. You could have a set of exemplar words that the child could select from to illustrate the phoneme.

The same principle can be applied to a game of bingo.

Game 4: Onset and rime match
Aim: to support the ability to hear sounds and synthesise these into a word

Resources required: a set of onsets, either single consonant or blends/digraphs (not strings at this stage) and a set of rimes.

Examples of this might be onsets of C, M, H, L, P, Sl, Pr, Sh.

Rimes might include ap, am, ip, ot, en, up, op. Do not use more complicated rimes such as ark or ight at this stage.

How to play
Place all onsets on the table face down. Deal five rimes to each child and place the rest in a pile face down. Each child has their set of rimes face up.

The first player takes an onset card and attempts to make a word by adding to one of their rimes. They say the onset and the rime and try to put them together. If they cannot, they put the onset back on the table. Next child takes a turn. Play proceeds until one child has been able to complete five matches of onset with rime and say the words.

Extension activity. Instead of completing with five words, each time a word is made the child takes a new rime from the pile to keep their total in front of them at five. Play proceeds until all rimes have been taken and the winner is the child with most words matched and read.

Differentiation. You could make this game harder by using strings and more complicated rimes such as *ark*, *ight*, etc., once children are capable of making the simple onset rime match.

Game 6: Cloze
Aim: to support the ability to select a word according to context and make use of phonics; make meaning out of a sentence

Resources required: single words for completing the story with some minimal pairs. Several baseboards with well-known rhymes or stories on them, with some words missing.

How to play
This game is similar to bingo but is used to focus children's attention on word detail and meaning.

Give each child a baseboard and place all of the word cards on the table.

Make sure each child is familiar with the story or rhyme they are working with. The first child reads their first sentence to the first gap and then scans the table to see if they can find the word to fill the gap. When they have completed the gap, play moves to the second child and so on around the table. When play returns to the first child, reread for them, or they read the first sentence again and then read on to the next gap when they scan the table to see if they can fill the gap. Play proceeds in this way until a child has completed their story or rhyme.

Example of story board

Once upon a .... Little ....
Riding Hood went for a walk.
On the way she met a wolf.
When she .... to her
grandma's house she knocked
.... the door.
'Come..........' said a voice.
When she went in her
grandma was in ....

You will see you do not need to have the whole story for this to be effective. The child can continue by telling the end of the story if reading it would be too much at this stage. The words deleted at this stage are obvious and phonically regular. At a later stage you can move to less obvious words such as deleting 'for' or visual words.

Note the story board has a double edge with a visible demarcation of the story on the page. This helps children with their focus and should also be used in writing to demarcate the writing area.

Minimal pairs for word selection might be time and tim, Red and bed, house and horse. It is important to use a whole text here rather than just sentences as it is the full text which adds meaning to the individual words. Cloze procedures which rely on single sentences teach inappropriate concepts about reading.

Visual strategies/look and say games

Visual recognition is the basis for automatic reading. It is important to build up a bank of words recognised on sight, which enables children to read fluently, without having to pay attention to decoding the word. This will also maintain meaning so that on occasions when they do need to pay attention to decoding the word there are other strategies such as meaning or analogy which can assist with the phonic analysis. To develop this instant recognition and fluency, children who have dyslexia need more practice than other children. They need to develop automaticity, which takes a lot of practice. However, many children who are dyslexic have a poor memory for sequence and orientation and many words are visually similar.

There are several sub-skills involved in memorising words. These include the following.

- The ability to recognise both the general sequence of letters and the orientation of letters.
- The ability to differentiate between visually similar words such as horse and house.
- The ability to remember the exact sequence of letters in words such as quite and quiet.
- The ability to assign a correct pronunciation to a visual stimulus dependent on context, for example live and live, (*she will live in a house, it was a live show*) present and present (*it was a thoughtful present he was given, she had to present her work*).

The following games improve the ability to remember visual detail. Again it is helpful if you teach reading sight words along with spelling so that the children are seeing the connection between the two and gaining with double practice.

Game 1: Visual word dominoes
Aim: to develop visual memory for sequence

Resources required: a set of domino cards with vocabulary that is visual and high-frequency words such as though, tough where, the, my, friends. These words need to be repeated several times over on different cards so that a core of around ten words is duplicated on 40 domino cards in different combinations.

How to play
Deal the cards seven to each player and put the rest in a pile face down. Place one card on the floor as the start card. The first child to play examines their cards to see if they can match the word and say the word on either end of the start card. If they cannot go, they pick up another card from the pile. Play moves to the next child to see if they can match and say the word and so on. The winner is the first child to get rid of their cards.

Game 2: Quick find word
Aim: to develop quick recognition strategies

Resources required: word cards with chosen words printed on, multiple copies of a text.

How to play
Give each child a text, this can be as simple or as difficult as needed according to the reading ability of the children. Read through the text with them first so they know what the text is about.

Hold up a word card and ask them to find this word on their text as quickly as possible. When they have identified it correctly they can collect the card. Repeat until all word cards have gone. The winner is the one with the most collected word cards who also has to read them back.

Variation
Place all the word cards on the table and the children have to collect them as quickly as possible – or you can give them a highlighter pen and they have to highlight every time a word occurs on the page and keep a tally.

Focus on meaning activities

Once children can recognise or decode words and retain these in memory, they need to develop the capacity to recognise when a word they think they have read correctly does not make sense or fit with what they know of the text. This involves 'listening' to the reading as well as a certain amount of stamina and self-correction. The following activities are designed to focus children's attention on the meaning of text and to listening to what makes sense and what doesn't.

Game 1: Create a story
Aim: to develop the concept of sequence and story

Resources required: a story written in clear sentences or a set of instructions with which the children would be familiar.

How to play
Print each sentence of the story or instruction on a strip of card.

Divide the cards among the children. The child who can identify the first sentence starts. Play proceeds around the table. The next child reads their sentences to see if they have the next sentence in the sequence. When the sequence is complete, the person completing it reads the whole story to make sure it is sensible.

Variation
Provide pairs of children with whole texts cut into sentences and time them to see who can complete the text most quickly. Watch to see how they complete it, whether one child is dominant, whether girls approach the tasks in different ways from boys.

Game 2: Listen carefully
Aim: to improve focus on meaning and accuracy

Resources required: text at an appropriate reading level for the children, counters.

How to play
Give the child a copy of the text to be read and instruct them that you are going to read the text but that sometimes you make mistakes, day-dream or get lost on what you are reading and you want them to keep track of what you are reading.

Start to read and after about two sentences misread either the odd word or a whole phrase. If the child picks this up give them a counter; if not, you have a counter. With several children it is the quickest one to pick up the mistake.

Variations
Get the children to highlight text they think you have read incorrectly. If your copy is high-lighted they can self-check.

Other activities and resources to assist in the teaching of reading

There are many activities which support the key areas of phonics, look and say and context. These activities can be found in texts designed specifically for this purpose or in comics and puzzle books. If you use the latter, children will automatically think the activity is a fun activity rather than a teaching one and engage with it more readily. Word searches, puzzles and spot-the-difference puzzles all assist in the core skills required to be good at remembering patterns and seeing single pieces as part of an overall picture.

PRACTICAL TASK PRACTICAL TASK **PRACTICAL TASK** PRACTICAL TASK **PRACTICAL TASK**

Buy two identical comics suitable for the age range you have had most experience with or for the age group of your next placement. Examine the story cartoons to see if you can make any into an activity such as those above; for example, a sequencing activity or a cloze using cartoon strips. You need two copies in order to use both faces of the page. Adapt any other activities in the comic such as find the differences, laminate and trial with some children.

Evaluate which strategies are brought to bear on the activities.

Hyperlexia

No chapter on reading with reference to dyslexia would be complete without some mention of the strange phenomenon of hyperlexia. Hyperlexic children are often overlooked and not diagnosed as dyslexic because they are generally competent in the areas which usually mark a child as dyslexic, they are competent at phonics, can memorise words well so will pass reading tests and spelling tests. The real difficulty lies in extracting or constructing meaning. They will read words in a sentence as if each is disconnected from the next and not create meaning from a sentence of words. They will have extreme difficulty with creating meaningful texts in writing. Their writing will often be a string of disconnected words using only the main content words of a piece of writing and missing the function words. The child will be able to tell you what their writing is supposed to say but be unable to read it because of its disjointed nature. They will read a piece but be unable to tell you what it was about and only be able to answer literal questions using key words as signals of what they are looking for. They are unable to use information from reading for a useful purpose. These children are at a real disadvantage because they often do not cause any alarm bells to ring and are often labelled as lazy or being awkward and unco-operative. These children need a lot of activities such as those for focusing on meaning above and proofreading activities to focus them on the process of reading and writing. They need less tuition on the basics of reading and spelling as this is something they are often good at.

Case Study

Darren thought he could read but often misread words, not picking up when his reading made no sense and he had little ability to 'decode' new words when he met them. He had no idea of meaning and thought as long as he 'read' a series of words in order, this counted as reading. This was allowed to continue for a number of years with his reading books but the demands of reading in the wider curriculum soon presented difficulties in Key Stage 2.

Darren needed to be taught strategies to check word accuracy, strategies to decode new words and to focus on meaning.

We started with some games to focus his attention on word form, we played minimal pairs and word-changing games. We also checked his grapheme/phoneme knowledge and plugged any gaps there. We focused on the number of sounds he could hear in words and how these were represented. We played word-changing games where each letter was changed in turn to form a new word. This often took the form of a competition, timing him against himself. He enjoyed challenging me to see if I could guess a letter to change his word. This improved not only his reading but his spelling too. Each time we did this we also wrote the words and thought of sentences they could fit into, focusing on the form and meaning of the word. We built up a collection of words he had learnt from these lessons. After a couple of months of this sort of basic tuition we moved on to meaning and whole-text work with the focus now less on each word and more on the overall meaning.

We undertook activities which looked at how sentences fit together and different meanings to texts could be constructed dependent on the choice of words. We would play games where I would read an incorrect detail from the text while he followed and he was expected to spot the error and vice versa, the object being to catch each other out. We also used a tape recorder to record first attempts, practice attempts and final renditions. In this way Darren was prompted to reflect on his own reading and how to improve it.

We expanded his reading to include texts from across the curriculum and away from his 'reading book'. We used instructional texts for science and maths that required that he follow instructions exactly and he had to read precisely. This often involved a lot of practical activities, something Darren liked and didn't link with the hard work of reading. In this context reading became incidental to the real task of carrying out an experiment.

Within a year he had brought his reading age up to the norm and was reading with more confidence across the curriculum. He still had some progress to make in terms of speed and fluency including intonation, but he could now at least use reading for a purpose.

A SUMMARY OF **KEY POINTS**

> Reading is a complex task requiring core skills – check hearing and sight as well as basic knowledge of alphabet names and sounds. Check core concepts such as letter, word and sentence boundaries.

> Reading involves both phonic and visual abilities as well as a good understanding of how texts make sense. Make sure you are not ignoring one aspect in favour of another. Make sure you have a good balance of these.

> Reading needs a lot of practice for dyslexic children to improve; you need to provide sufficient practice in as many contexts as possible and of a variety of genres.

> You need a good understanding yourself of when and how to prompt a child to use an appropriate strategy, whether this is phonics, look and say, analogy or context. Make sure your own knowledge is excellent.

> You should aim to provide different ways for all children in the class to practise so that the dyslexic children do not feel 'special' in any negative way.

MOVING *ON* > > > > > > MOVING *ON* > > > > > > MOVING *ON*

Evaluate how many reading tasks in the classroom are genuine reading tasks and how many are constructed for the purposes of tuition. Try to find real reasons for reading which require specific skills such as reading instructions which require precise reading. Observe how many reading opportunities are missed during a school day because a teacher provides material which they then read for the children; this might include worksheets, instructions or information in a book, notices, etc. How many of these could be planned into 'reading practice' for some children?

REFERENCES REFERENCES **REFERENCES** REFERENCES **REFERENCES** REFERENCES

Bryant, P, Bradley, L, MacLean, M, and Crossland, D (1989) Nursery rhymes, phonological skills and reading. *Journal of Child Language*, 16: 407–28

Connors, M (2007) No one strategy is best for teaching reading, professor shows, *ScienceDaily (Jan. 26, 2007) at* www.sciencedaily.com/releases/2007/01/070125173154.htm (accessed 13/2/08)

Dyslexia Contact Magazine, 27 (3) September 2008. Bracknell: BDA

Ehri, L (1997) Learning to read and learning to spell are one and the same, almost, in Perfetti, C, Rieben, L and Fayol, M (eds) *Learning to spell: research theory and practice across languages (pp237–69),* Mahwah, NJ: Erlbaum

Goswami, U (1999) Causal connections in beginning reading; the importance of rhyme. *Journal of Research in Reading*, 22: 217–40

Goswami, U and Bryant, P (1990) *Phonological skills and learning to read*. Hove: Psychology Press

Goswami, U and Ziegler, J (2006) A developmental perspective on the neural code for written words. *Trends in Cognitive Sciences*, 10 (4): 142–5

Petty, G (2004) *Teaching today*. Cheltenham: Nelson Thornes

Plowden, M (1967) *The Plowden Report: Children and their primary schools. A report of the Central Advisory Council for Education*. London: HMSO

Pollock, J and Waller, E (2001) *Day-to-day dyslexia in the classroom*. Abingdon: RoutledgeFalmer

Rose, J (2004) *Independent review of the teaching of early reading.* Nottingham: DfES

Wyse, D and Styles, M (2007) Synthetic phonics and the teaching of reading: the debate surrounding England's 'Rose Report'. *Literacy*, (41) (1) April 2007

7

Mathematics and dyslexia

Chapter objectives

By the end of this chapter you should be aware of:

- the skills necessary to teach the core skills of addition and multiplication;
- the difficulties many dyslexic children encounter in trying to learn multiplication and addition;
- a variety of games and activities which will teach and provide opportunities to practise these key elements of mathematics;
- the importance of presentation of mathematics problems.

This chapter addresses the following Professional Standards for QTS:

Q10, Q12, Q14, Q17, Q19, Q22, Q23, Q25 (a), (b), (d), Q26 (a), (b), Q29.

Introduction

While the stereotype of a dyslexic person is someone who cannot spell or read, it is becoming recognised that mathematical ability is also often affected in dyslexia. This is often called dyscalculia. The reason mathematical thinking and reasoning may be affected is that the same parts of the brain are being used in mathematical operations and the same short-term and working memory are needed as in reading and spelling. Sometimes it is only mathematics that is affected and as a trainee teacher you may not think the child has dyslexia because they can read and spell with reasonable accuracy. It is still well worth screening or having the child assessed for the core deficits which mark the dyslexic profile to find out if this lack of attainment in mathematics may be because of dyslexia.

Theoretical background

Mathematics is an area of difficulty for many children with dyslexia. It is sometimes subsumed as an aspect of dyslexia or it may be defined as dyscalculia. The severity of the difficulties encountered can be from a slight difficulty in remembering tables and being slow in working out number bonds to severe difficulty and being totally incapable of working out most mathematical problems beyond simple addition.

The main areas affected in mathematics are as follows.

- Remembering multiplication tables.
- Remembering or working out division.
- Being able to work out number bonds in addition.
- Being able to work out number bonds in subtraction.
- Place value.
- Writing the correct answer but presenting it incorrectly, with transposition of numbers.
- Telling the time, especially analogue time.
- Working out time lapses.

- Vocabulary associated with mathematics.
- Reading mathematics problems embedded within narrative contexts.

Henderson (2000) also includes the following.

- Understanding fractions.
- Understanding percentages.
- Use of a calculator.
- Recognising the use of the decimal point.
- Estimation using formulae.

There are many people who are not dyslexic who have difficulty particularly with remembering their tables but they generally have a way of referring to known key tables or techniques for working out answers, even if this is by resorting to saying their tables. Dyslexic children have greater difficulty because they very often cannot remember the key answers from which to work out other answers; they do not remember the tables to 'chant' them and once stressed by not being able to recall the answer, their memory often goes completely blank and fails to assist them in any of these other strategies. The problem with mathematics is that it relies on two elements: memory and/or understanding. Chinn (1998) identifies that memory and stress, when memory fails, can cause an early sense of failure. Even if you understand how to add up tens and units when shown, you have to remember how to do it the next time and it is not uncommon for dyslexic children to forget the method between teaching sessions or to overgeneralise.

Short-term and working memory are areas of deficit in dyslexic children. For efficient recall of tables most people need to use or practise the skill or it is lost. This is magnified a hundred-fold with dyslexic children. They need far more practice than other children, but because we are not continually using tables in the same way we continually use reading, they are liable to be forgotten much more easily.

In order to provide sufficient practice every session, even if the main teaching is about shape, should start with a quick game to reinforce the core components of maths tables or number bonding.

The other difficulty some dyslexic children have is when they know the answer but write it in reverse order, thus recording an incorrect answer. So they work out that 9 times 3 is 27 but write 72. With spelling, getting a word near enough so that the reader knows what the word is may suffice but in mathematics the answer is just wrong. How are you as a teacher to know they meant 27 but wrote it backwards rather than they just cannot work out the answer and wrote 72 as a wild guess instead?

There is a further problem with maths, particularly with Key Stage 2: a lot of mathematical problems are embedded within word problems that the child cannot read or they forget what the problem is about in trying to decode the reading aspect of it. Aspects of layout will be outlined later in this chapter.

Addition

All children need to be able to conserve before they can add up, they need to be able to count and match one to one so that as they move one counter they count only one counter, not move two counters but only count one. This is a very basic step and may need extra time with dyslexic children but this is not usually an area of great difficulty. The first difficulties generally arise in what is often called 'counting on' in addition when using numbers to represent the amounts rather than using only counters. The problem 4 + 5 may present the challenge that the child can read 4 and put out four counters, they can read 5 and put out five counters but they either forget the process of what is involved or try to rely on memory or guesswork to know the answer. If you introduce the concept of counting on from 4 they often then forget that they are adding on 5 more or forget when to stop. The process of counting on from the larger number, especially if the smaller number is presented first, also eludes them.

Game to practise and improve the ability to count on

Game 1: Counting on hats
Aim: to teach children to count on from a known quantity rather than starting at 1

Resources required: paper hats with the number written the right way around on one side (back) and in mirror writing on the front of the hat. Sticky patches so that you can change numbers easily are a good idea. A set of counters with sticky patches (felt used to be used for this because it stuck to itself; if this cannot be found any number of sticky substances may be used). A mirror, baseboard for the game, counting on cards, dice.

Activity
Present the problem for the child. Always present the problem with the larger number first to start with. Ask them to identify the correct hat (which has the number presented the correct way around for them at this stage); with a problem such as 5 + 4 they select the hat with the 5 on it. You now put the hat on the child's head with the reversed number showing so that when the child looks in the mirror the number 5 appears the right way around for them.

You now tell the child they have *5 in the head and can count on*. At this stage you may ask them to pick up four more counters and put on the sticky patches on the hat. Now help them to count on from 5, counting the extra counters until they get to 9. Because they have something to touch or look at they are more likely to stop once you get to 9.

Moving on
Once they have the idea of putting the extra counters on the hat you can keep them on the table for them to count.

Moving on again
Once they have 5 in the head you can ask them to put up four fingers on which to count. Gradually they get the idea of the larger (first) number being in the head.

Moving on to playing the game
At this point you can play the game using a baseboard which has a track across it with every third or fourth place an instruction to take a counting on card. The card has a problem on it which the child has to answer. If they get it wrong they go back two places.

The baseboard can be made as easy or complicated, as visually stimulating or as simple as you wish.

An error of recording or wrong thinking and processing?

In order that children can manipulate numbers quickly they need to realise that it makes no difference if you add 5 onto 4 or 4 onto 5, the answer is the same. In order to do this you will need to take a few steps back and set out number problems in sets such as a set of 4, and a set of 5. You can move the sets around the table. Ask the child to stand on different sides of the table and keep repeating the exercise until they realise that it makes no difference whether they are looking at 4 + 5 or 5 + 4, the answer is the same. They can then manipulate the permutations in their mind, so seeing 4 + 5 they automatically reverse the problem.

Once this sort of basic problem is addressed, there are other challenges when you introduce vertical addition, especially with tens and units. We spend a great deal of time ensuring children know we read left to right in reading but then have to reverse this when we add up with tens and units. Furthermore some practices of splitting the tens from the units in mental mathematics starters to help most children, totally confuse dyslexic children. There are many schools which teach that the easy way to add 25 and 32 is to add the tens together to produce 50 and then add the units to make 7 and put the two answers together to total 57. This is not only the reverse of what we do when we write the sum down but puts too much pressure on memory for most dyslexic children. However, you can guarantee that if they do remember anything they will remember to add the tens first and carry this over into written calculations.

It is not uncommon either for Key Stage 2 children to confuse the process for multiplication with addition and add diagonally when they have been introduced to multiplication.

By examining the errors children make you will often see where the problem lies.

An example of this type of error can be seen in the following sum:

```
  35
+ 24
= 68
```

Or even 86

Or 77

Can you spot how these errors have occurred?

The first answer is created by adding the top line horizontally and placing the answer in the units column then adding the bottom line horizontally and putting the answer in the tens column, so at least this child knows to record their answer right to left.

The second answer is created by the same addition but by placing the answer to the top line in the tens column and the answer to the bottom line in the units or even by adding the bottom line before the top line.

The third possibility is created by adding diagonally.

Once you start with calculations that require an answer greater than 9 in the units column the difficulties are endless.

BEEFECIIAE IVSK

REFLECTIVE TASK

Consider the possible wrong answers to the following addition. What processes are used to achieve such answers? Compare your answers with those of a fellow trainee or class teacher.

$$
\begin{array}{r}
65 \\
+23 \\
\hline
=
\end{array}
$$

Multiplication

Multiplication brings its own challenges in the variety of ways children can produce a wrong answer but by actually still knowing their multiplication tables.

Calculations such as

$$
\begin{array}{r}
28 \\
\times 32
\end{array}
$$

can produce answers such as 244, when the 2 has been multiplied diagonally with the 2 and the 3 diagonally with the 8. You will see that the actual calculations of $2 \times 2 = 4$ and $3 \times 8 = 24$ giving 244 indicate that this child knows their tables but not the process for computing and recording the correct answer. It would be very easy though to assume this child does not know their tables.

A wrong answer does not always mean they don't know their tables. It is very frustrating for a child who knows their tables to continually get the answer wrong because they do not know or understand the process or rules of recording answers.

Check the child knows their basic tables by playing the following games.

Game 2: Dartboard mathematics
Aim: to develop and practise the ability to add or multiply

Resources required: a laminated wipe-clean 'dartboard'.
Either counters to push, or small objects to throw (two per player).
Tokens to collect for correct answers.

(for subtraction activities a set of cards to place on the table which are used to subtract the lower number from).

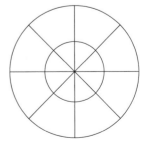

Your dartboard should be sectioned to allow you to write the numbers you are dealing with at that point in time.

Write the numbers you want to practise and decide on the rule, either addition or multiplication.

How to play

Addition – use two counters and throw/push the counters until they land on different sections of the board and add the two numbers together.

Multiplication – there are several ways of playing this game. You could decide that whatever number the player lands on is multiplied by 2 or 3 or whatever is the chosen number table to work with, or you can use two counters for random multiplication – multiplying the two numbers that the counters land on.

The first player throws or pushes their first counter so that it lands on a section of the board; if you are using only the 3 times table they multiply this number by 3, if correct they collect a token.

Play goes to the next player.

If using random multiplication your player would use two counters and multiply the two numbers on which they land.

Unfortunately this game does not work so well for division or subtraction.

Game 3: Addition and multiplication pairs

Aim: to teach and reinforce memory of number bonds/tables and equivalent calculations

Resources required: sets of cards which total to the same answer. For example, 3 + 3, 5 + 1, 2 + 4, or for multiplication:- 3 × 4, 2 × 6, 12 × 1.

Cards that stand up add a bit of difference to this game but are not essential.

Answer cards bearing the total number such as 8, 16, 20.

You need to be able to work with several sets of number bonds or tables for this game and it works best with pairs of children.

How to play:

Hold up an answer card bearing the total number such as 20, challenge the children to be the first to identify a calculation that totals to this number. When the first child identifies a correct card such as 10 + 10 or 4 × 5, ask them how many more they can see that also total this amount. Allow them a minute or so to collect all the cards they can.

The other child may now be hopping up and down eager to find the others (having been given a start by their opponent). If the first player does not find all the cards within the time allowed, let the other player complete the process.

It is then their turn – you hold up a card bearing an answer and they have to find the cards which make this answer.

Once children are familiar with and competent with addition alone and multiplication alone, you can introduce both into the same game.

A variation of this is Bingo where the baseboard has the answer on it and small cards bear a calculation which would total to that answer.

Lawton (2006) provides a comprehensive outline of mathematical errors encountered in children's work and how these occur as well as how to address them and this text is recommended to you for further research in this area.

The vocabulary of mathematics

Mathematics has a language of its own which is not often encountered outside the maths lesson other than in science or has a different meaning to that in other contexts. Vocabulary which may pose problems includes words such as equation, product, words where there are several synonyms such as plus, add, sum, etc.

You also need to consider the practical examples and use of language which children encounter in everyday life. For example, at home when children are asked if they would like some more beans on their dinner, they actually get less than they did the first time; when sharing out the cake someone who has a large piece still has a piece smaller than the remaining cake unless of course you are cutting into the last half of the cake; some children are told they can watch TV 'in a minute' only to have to wait half an hour; some parents use the colloquial *yes you can do that now in a minute*.

Dyslexic children already have difficulty with vocabulary; the added difficulty of grappling with the concept of maths, the memory demands and the vocabulary of maths can prove too much for some children. You should always be aware of the difficulty of mathematical vocabulary and how this can turn an otherwise difficult problem into an impossible one.

Some of the difficulties children encounter are related to the many and varied words associated with maths, for example:

Add, total, sum, plus, and
subtract, take away, minus, less.

PRACTICAL TASK PRACTICAL TASK **PRACTICAL TASK** PRACTICAL TASK **PRACTICAL TASK**

Devise a game to teach the various words associated with mathematics. This may be a bingo game, dominoes, snap or a more adventurous game. Remember the outcome is that the children will know that several words can mean the same thing. The outcome is not just to recognise the words.

Using your teaching assistant

The use of your teaching assistant is worth considering in relation to maths. This can be not just in relation to supporting activities but to act as an objective observer to assess, note and evaluate any difficulties or misconceptions. Your teaching assistant may pick up on misconceptions when as a teacher you may not notice them because you are so engrossed in the activity with the child. As discussed (Chapter 3), you need to support and plan your use of your teaching assistant.

You do need to make sure that your teaching assistant is using the correct vocabulary and not confusing the issue further, that they are using the same methods as you (not what they remember from their own schooling) and that they are able to analyse a difficulty and move the activity on, in the appropriate direction or that they are representing the problem in a different format without making it either more difficult or too easy.

Morgan (2006) identifies the following ways in which the teaching assistant can support maths with pupils:

- Working with a focus group to keep them on track, repeating information.
- Supporting pupils using specific resources.
- Encouraging pupils to answer questions, creating a 'can do' atmosphere.
- Carrying out assessments planned by the teacher through observation of the pupil and activity.
- Modelling an activity or recording the answer for the pupil.

Intervention programmes

There are many intervention programmes published by the government as part of the Numeracy Strategy but not all of these are suitable for dyslexic children as they are premised on the basis of usual development and they group all children having difficulties together. So you could have children who may be having difficulty due to more complex reasons such as dyslexia and scotopic sensitivity syndrome with children who are having difficulty with basic concepts and are of lower ability.

The National Numeracy Strategy (DfEE 1999a, b) lists several reasons why children may make mistakes, including the following.

- Computational errors.
- Careless mistakes.
- Misconceptions.
- Wrong operation used.
- Overgeneralisation of a rule.
- Undergeneralisation of a rule.
- Random response.
- Incomplete concept formation or gaps in understanding.

Dyslexic children, as mentioned, also have the difficulty of short-term and working memory deficit which even if they understand the process hinders their ability to complete the process. Short-term memory refers to the memory used to retain information or facts for a short time. For example, short-term memory would be used in remembering the numbers and operation in 4 + 3. Working memory is the memory used to actually process this information into an answer. Add these difficulties to the list above and you will see that mathematics is a particular difficulty for some dyslexic children.

Motivation is crucial in teaching mathematics. It does not have the immediate usefulness that reading does. It is not something that children see modelled by parents in the way reading might be and for some children it is literally like a foreign language. Some children find fascination in mathematics, however, this is not very common with dyslexic children. How to provide motivation and enough practice to allow dyslexic children to over-learn and develop automaticity is a difficulty for many teachers who cannot see beyond the worksheet or mathematics scheme textbook.

Games can form the motivation and focus for children experiencing difficulties with mathematics and assist in memory training. There may be the need for more functional prompt material (such as 10- or 100-squares or number lines) in order to keep play going. However, it is the play which provides the practice which is so essential to dyslexic children.

Essential resources for mathematics games
Wipe-clean boards, dry-wipe pens
Bits of card
Sticky patches
Counters
Timer
Dice (either electronic or traditional)
100-squares
Copies of multiplication tables and number bonds

Games to reinforce and practise all four rules of mathematics

Game 4: Dominoes
Aim: to practise the four rules

Resources required: a set of dominoes with both calculations and answers on using the number bonds or tables you are working with. Wipe-clean blank dominoes allow you to write your own numbers on without having a lot of different sets of dominoes. The cards need to be large: about 15 cm each card, so that you can play on the floor. The size of the card assists in lack of distraction because the numbers are well spaced.

Prompt card of tables to help them identify correct answers.

How to play
Deal seven cards to each player and place the remainder in a pile.

Place a start card from the pile on the floor, and invite each player to see if they can match one of the ends of this first card.

The player matches any card they can which is correct and picks another card from the pile to retain seven cards. If they cannot go, they still pick another card from the pile thus increasing the number of cards they have.

The winner is the first to get rid of all of their cards or the one with least cards if they both are unable to go.

All of the previous games and teaching of the four rules can be adapted to activities such as bingo, snap, dominoes, find the pair, etc.

Other strategies and resources

Colour charts for tables
Using information from art can assist in helping some children with tables. By using primary colours for certain tables and combining those colours, a child can be assisted in realising the components that make up other tables. For example, if you use yellow for the 2 times table and red for 3 then you can create 5 in orange; if you colour code 4 blue then you can also create the 6 times table in green (2 = yellow and 4 = blue, put them together to make green/6).

Another strategy is that if a child knows their 2 times tables they should be able to work out their 4 times table by doubling the answer. Just colour-coding tables for individual preference can also help with many children regardless of any clever coding and colour mixing.

Fascinating studies with synaesthetes (*Horizon* at BBC website) show that many people do actually see numbers in colours. Cuisenaire rods used the same principle to assist with teaching of mathematics, particularly number bonding. Emerson and Horner (2008) support the use of Stern's structural arithmetic, which uses a similar concept of colour coding a certain number stick so that children can see the colour combinations and how they bond to 10.

There is some evidence that music can help with remembering information required in maths as well as the conceptual development in maths. (BBC online 1999; songsfor teaching.com).

More complicated problems

Fractions

Fractions pose a particular difficulty for dyslexic children both in relation to the concept and in relation to the vocabulary. As the fraction represents a smaller and smaller quantity, the number used gets larger, which can be particularly confusing. So even when using concrete examples such as a cake: if you halve it you represent this as ½; as the pieces become smaller, for example ¼ or ⅛, the numbers used get larger. You also get more portions in front of you. Even logical attempts to explain fractions can run foul of children's reasoning. When a child was asked if they would rather have ¼ (1 out of 4 pieces of the cake) or ⅛ (1 out of 8 pieces) they answered ⅛; reasoning that if they wanted to come back for more there were more pieces left (7) than if they had ¼, which would only leave 3 pieces. It is very difficult to argue against this type of logic.

Time

Telling the time, finding time differences and calculations can all prove difficult for a dyslexic child when using analogue clocks and watches. Digital time proves less difficult but can often be confusing to the child when they are converting from digital time to analogue time and vice versa.

The vocabulary of time is also a challenge as it uses terms which may not have been encountered in other aspects of maths or may still be proving difficult in maths. Terms such as 'quarter past', 'half past', 'quarter to' may seem strange. Many children are not sure which side of the clock is 'past' and which is 'to'; why at a certain time change the point of reference from numbers (5 past, 10 past) to fractions? There is also interchangeable terminology for long/minute hand and short/hour hand. Some teachers use the term 'big hand'. You need to make sure that you use the correct terminology and that you are consistent. Shifting from 'long hand' to 'minute hand' can be confusing and if you use the four terms long/short, minute/hour, some children may expect there to be four hands on the clock, since some clocks have a third ('second') hand, this reinforces such misconceptions.

Try to use a clock which has only two hands and which is geared so that the hands move in synchrony with each other. Colour one-half of the clock red for past. Timex produced a very successful watch for children using this technique with the quarters marked on it as well. This will assist children in determining which is 'minutes past' and which is 'minutes to'. You need a context which forces children in a fun way to constantly tell the time and to use the growing knowledge they have.

Apart from constantly asking children to tell the time and to calculate what the time will be in five minutes or to keep an eye on the clock and tell you when to stop an activity at half-past ten you can play games which effectively work this knowledge.

The following game can be adapted for whatever difficulty level you wish depending on which aspects of time you need to practise.

Game 5: Time travel
Aim: to practise telling the time

Resources required: a board with hexagonal stones to 'cross' the board (this can be downloaded off the internet). http://mathworld.wolfram.com/HexagonalGrid.html
Random stones on the board should have a 'take a yellow/red/blue card' instruction on them
Counters
Die
Problem cards
Watch
Paper and pen for working out

How to play
Each player places their counter on one side of the board; the aim of the game is to get to the other side as quickly as possible.

Each player throws the die and jumps the number of stones indicated. If they land on a stone instructing them to take a card, they do so and complete the task on the card. If they are not correct they go back to their original position.

Instructions on the card can include adding on minutes to a clock, drawing a clock face with a designated time on it, converting digital time to analogue time. The instructions are relevant to the child's level of development and teaching.

Children particularly like 'wild cards' which allow another child to make up a problem for their opponent.

Adapting other games used here to a time focus
The games detailed for addition can also be used for time; games such as bingo, dominoes, snap, etc., can all reinforce equivalent time activities.

Layout

Many dyslexic children are disadvantaged because the teacher has not paid attention to layout.

Difficulties occur when there is too much information on a page, mathematics problems are embedded in a problem the child has to read, or the print is too small and dense for the child to be able to decipher.

Helping children by thoughtful layout:

- Use font 14 bold, use cream or other off-white colour sheets.
- Space the problems out so that there are only a few problems on a page with good spacing between them.

Make sure that the child is only being presented with a mathematics challenge, not a reading challenge as well.

If working from a textbook where the problems are presented close together, cover any other text apart from the current problem, with a sheet of plain white paper, or use a card mask with a section cut out to reveal only the appropriate text.

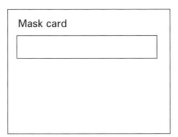

Mask card

Using games to develop mathematical skills

CASE STUDY

Tim had incredible difficulty with remembering his tables. We practised them regularly but there was little improvement. After investigating the relationship between colour and memory, I asked him one day *What colour is the colour of your 8 times table?* He did not look at me strangely as I expected but immediately said *blue*. So we got the paint pots out and mixed as many shades of blue as we could think of. I then asked him which shade of blue 2 × 8 was and he pointed to light blue; 12 × 8 was the very darkest blue, nearly black. Without any prompting Tim outlined how in his mind's eye the 2 times table was shaded from light blue down to very dark blue. We drew up a table writing each line in a different shade of blue and asked him to hang it on his wall at home where he could see it often.

Within two weeks he knew his 8 times table and would refer to the shade of colour before answering. If I asked him what was the answer to 6 × 8 he would always refer to *seeing the colour half way down, a sort of mid greeny blue* and then give me the answer. It is interesting to note that this child had a good visual memory when reading and was poor with phonics. His visual memory was obviously what assisted him in memorising his tables but he needed that extra bit of stimulation that the colour brought. We coloured each of the tables a different colour with different shades and started to refer to the tables as the red set of 6s, which he also found difficult, the yellow 3s, etc. Within six weeks he knew every table by reference to the colour. I am not saying this will work with every child; the important issue here is finding something that works for each and every individual child.

Principles for playing games
- Revise what you think the children already know and make sure there are no misconceptions.
- Teach and practise one function systematically.
- Introduce the reciprocal relation such as subtraction from addition by referring back to the base rule.
- Use multisensory techniques and concrete meaningful examples as much as possible to reinforce your main mode of teaching.
- Use games regularly and often to reinforce what has been taught.

Hints for using game cards
- Children with dyslexia may also be dyspraxic, experiencing manipulation difficulties. Wind rubber bands around the edge of playing cards in order to give extra grip.
- Some children may need matt lamination to minimise glare. If you cannot get matt you could spray your card with hairspray – when this dries it leaves a matt finish.
- Use at least 14-point bold text, preferably dark brown or blue in colour on cream-coloured card. This addresses the needs of both dyslexic children and children with scotopic sensitivity syndrome, which is often co-morbid with dyslexia.

REFLECTIVE TASK

Observe a child who has difficulty with an aspect of maths, and analyse where the difficulty lies. Is it a difficulty with knowledge or a difficulty with processes? What is the small step needed to get them over this 'hump'? This process is called tracking back. Look it up on the TDA website, www.tda.gov.uk.

PRACTICAL TASK PRACTICAL TASK PRACTICAL TASK PRACTICAL TASK PRACTICAL TASK

Design a game to teach time. Consider what other knowledge or skills are required to play the game. What reading demands are there in the game?

A SUMMARY OF **KEY POINTS**

> Mathematics relies heavily on memory and dyslexic children need concrete materials more than other children so that they can literally see the problem.
> Mathematical problems should be stripped of extraneous information so that the child only has to deal with the maths, not with decoding a problem embedded in words.
> Mathematics is best retained if used frequently for a purpose.
> Games provide practice and motivation; use them as often as possible.

MOVING *ON* > > > > > > MOVING *ON* > > > > > > MOVING *ON*

Look at the resource texts used to teach mathematics, evaluate what assumptions lie behind the text and problems presented. Is your own understanding of maths and the stages of learning sufficient to allow you to pinpoint areas of difficulty? Examine mathematics problems from the child's perspective; think of other ways of teaching the same content rather than using the textbook and traditional problems. Read some books written about children's errors such as those listed in the following References.

REFERENCES REFERENCES **REFERENCES** REFERENCES **REFERENCES** REFERENCES

BBC Online network (1999) Learning maths through music. http://news.bbc.co.uk/1/hi/education/ 297073.stm (accessed 17.3.08)

Chinn, S (1998) *Sum hope breaking the numbers barrier.* London: Souvenir Press

DfEE (1999a) *Professional development materials 3 and 4. Guide for your professional development Book 2: Raising standards in mathematics at Key Stage 2.* London: DfEE

DfEE (1999b) *Professional development materials 3 and 4. Guide for your professional development Book 3: Raising standards in mathematics at Key Stage 2.* London: DfEE

Emerson, J and Horner, V (2008) Dyslexia and mathematics. Can Stern's structural arithmetic materials help? *Dyslexia Contact*, 27 (3): September 2008

Henderson, A (2000) *Maths for the dyslexic. A practical guide.* London: David Fulton

Lawton, F (2006) Number, in Hansen, A (ed.) *Children's errors in mathematics.* Exeter: Learning Matters

Horizon (1999) 'Derek tastes of ear wax'. www.bbc.co.uk/sn/tvradio/programmes/horizon/derek_- trans.shtml

Morgan, D (2006) *Becoming a higher-level teaching assistant. Primary mathematics.* Exeter: Learning Matters

Useful websites

www.songsforteaching.com/mathsongs.htm Songs for teaching using music to promote learning

8
Using ICT

Chapter objectives

By the end of this chapter you should be aware of:

- **the skills necessary to teach and use ICT effectively with dyslexic pupils;**
- **difficulties of using ICT;**
- **the potential of using ICT to support and further other learning areas such as writing.**

This chapter addresses the following Professional Standards for QTS:

Q10, Q12, Q14, Q17, Q19, Q22, Q23, Q25(a), (b), (d), Q26b.

Introduction

The use of ICT, particularly computers, is recognised as one of the most worthwhile and effective means of supporting children. However, children cannot just be expected to pick up the techniques for using laptops without tuition. Teachers may feel less confident about providing teaching in this area especially as each brand of computer/laptop is different and programs vary significantly. Too often children teach themselves to type and pick up unhelpful fingering or one-fingered typing techniques. Ofsted (1999) was quite emphatic in its recommendation that pupils using laptops or software packages *should receive specific teaching and be given opportunities to practise keyboard skills to improve their speed and accuracy*. Crivelli (2008) notes that although high-tech is appealing, often improving the use of 'low-tech' existing facilities is just as effective.

Theoretical background

ICT is one of the main resources available to dyslexic pupils. Many statements include the requirement that a laptop is available to the dyslexic child. Whether these pieces of equipment are used to their greatest advantage is often a matter of understanding and experience on the part of the teacher despite the National Curriculum entitlement of all children to ICT teaching. Often they are left in a cupboard because the teacher cannot be bothered with the hassle of supporting the pupil in using them if they are using adaptive software, or they are used until the pupil meets a difficulty, then they are abandoned. Using ICT requires several core areas of knowledge and understanding. It requires an understanding of the difficulties encountered by a dyslexic child in terms of literacy, organisation, understanding of different aspects of the syndrome and an understanding in terms of the difficulties faced by a dyslexic child when using ICT. It also requires an understanding of how to adapt and use different technologies for each child. Medwell et al. (2007a), pose the following question: *What is distinctive about electronic tests? What do children need to know about such texts in order to use them effectively, and what do you need to know in order to develop their knowledge?* This is a crucial question you need to reflect on when reading this chapter.

Different technologies

Photocopy and then complete the following grid.

	Computer word-processing facility	Spell-checker on computer	Hand-held spell-checker	Audio digital recorder
Function – how it can help				
Reading skills required				
Sub-skills of phonics required				
Sub-skills of Look and Say required				
Skill of comprehension required				
Skills of organisation required				

Now revisit this list and outline where you feel difficulties may lie considering what you have learnt in previous chapters about reading, writing, spelling, etc.

Different levels of using ICT

ICT can be used in a basic functional way to word-process work and check spellings. This is largely a simple editing process. It also, though, allows the opportunity and provides the motivation for purposeful and functional reading, selection of material, copying and pasting and creation of quite complex documents, all of which may well be beyond a dyslexic child if attempted in the traditional way with books and pen and paper. All of these are possible for the dyslexic child as long as their teachers know how to support them in this task and can anticipate the hurdles. It also encourages a risk-taking confidence within an environment that is non-judgemental and offers support. It is valuable therefore in the development of independence in dyslexic learners if used supportively.

When thinking more broadly, ICT also encompasses the use of multimedia equipment such as digital cameras, digital voice recorders, talking books and interactive use of ICT to engage with others at a distance. Skype is a fast-growing facility for talking on the telephone while using the internet.

Butteriss and Litterick (2008) draw our attention to the fact that most ICT/computers are located at a workstation or are used at home or in school. A useful list of mobile technology is available for the interested reader in their chapter in the new edition of *The Dyslexia Handbook 2008/9*, available from the British Dyslexia Association.

Reading electronic texts

Reading using ICT can range from reading DVD/CD-ROMs of well-known stories where the page is turned by the click of a button and characters can speak by highlighting text, to truly interactive reading using hyperlinked texts. You need to be comfortable and informed about the different types of reading from fiction to non-fiction and research-based reading in order to include these different genres in your planning. You should also become familiar with accessibility features on certain sites and teach children how to use them. These may include the ability to change the font size, type and colour, to change the background colour or have the text read for you. You need to make sure that the reading demands are within the capabilities of the children you are teaching. Reflect on the fact that most of the reading demands are often beyond the capabilities of many average readers and will pose extra difficulties to children with reading difficulties unless you allocate a teaching assistant to help the child, and this may include reading the text or showing them how to activate the accessibility functions. If you work with the teaching assistant, this then has implications for training them (see Chapter 3). Bearne et al. (2007) note that reading demands proliferate when reading on screen, stating that *they are likely to come across much material couched in formats more suitable for adults than children*.

Researching on the Internet

REFLECTIVE TASK

What do you use the Internet for? How many different formats are you presented with on the sites you visit? What skills do you need to navigate around them?

With text-to-speech and speech-to-text software the hard work may be taken out of composing and reading texts, but for children who have not been shown how to use the accessibility feature of most websites, reading a menu-driven site or accessing information can be a challenge not only for them but for their teachers too. Even when there is a text-reader feature, if the text has not been constructed properly then the reading can be bizarre and stilted. Try using the text reader on the ADSHE website (www.adshe.org.uk/) to experience some of the problems of text readers. The punctuation is in the wrong place for reading lists and if the mouse is moved at all, the reader returns to the beginning of the text to start reading again. This is a very frustrating website for using the text reader and it is not alone.

Reading on the net is a skill in itself for many children, which if they are not taught how to tackle it they may well give up on. Anderson (2007) comments that the reading skills required of the net are often nearer to adult level than children's level. You need to be able to note suitable sites to direct children to and to take the hard work out of researching on the net. This involves knowing the site yourself and knowing which parts of the menu to use to get to the information needed, as this is not always obvious. You also need to be able to help children when they get stuck. One way of coping with this is to pair a good experienced reader/researcher with a less competent or confident one. Using older pupils to help with this is a good idea and develops the social skills of older children as well as the ICT skills of younger children.

Research skills

When selecting websites or CD-ROMs/DVDs you should be aware that some are really only on-screen versions of a linear text and do not allow for flipping backwards and forwards or following links in the way a text which is hyperlinked can perform. Anderson (2007) is highly critical of many linear sites which hinder rather than help dyslexic pupils. Hyperlinking allows the child to jump from one source to another without the need to read through pages and pages of information that may be irrelevant; however, this linking around has to be taught. And the user has to know how to get back again and how to store favourite pages in their 'favourites' tab.

Using key words to search can be frustrating if the word is not spelt correctly, so if children are searching for topic work it is advisable to tell them to ask an adult to write it down for them. If you want children to research particular topics it is a good idea to have a few references ready to hand in order to help children if they get stuck. You also then need to know how to navigate your way around that particular site to find relevant information.

If your school is using a content screener which blocks adult content, you need to make sure that children can still access essential information. One theatre company was obtaining very few bookings from one local authority. It was found that their adverts were not getting into the school and no school could access their site for their forthcoming production of *Dick Whittington*.

Once children have learnt to access information at sites, they need to know how to copy and paste information or make notes in a Word document. For this they need to know how to have two windows open at once and how to move between them. This is a relatively easy task but does need explicit teaching to children.

They also of course need to know how to check the validity of a site in the same way they would check the authenticity of information from hard-copy texts.

Using interactive whiteboards

Interactive whiteboards (IWBs) are now commonplace in most classrooms and serve a pedagogical function in attracting and maintaining children's interest since these are the focus of attention rather than the teacher; however, you need to be aware of the negative aspects of using them. The most obvious is that many dyslexic children need to mark their place in text with a finger or ruler; this is impossible on IWBs where the text appears as just a mass of words. You need to be aware of this and to track the text for some children or use a laptop with the same text so that they can use a finger to read on screen. Other negative aspects include the following.

- Light reflection which is not only a problem with many non-dyslexic children but a significant problem for children with 'visual stress' or Irlen syndrome.
- Print/background contrast will need to be adjusted, as may the colour of font against background.
- The use of IWBs can lead to more information being given in written form when previously it may have been given orally. You need to be aware of the overuse of the IWB for your ease rather than for any pedagogical reason.
- Reliance on the IWB can be misplaced; there are many times when the technology does not work and you are left wondering what to do. You really need a back-up system in case of system failure.

Writing using ICT

Simple Microsoft Word documents

Word-processing reduces the labour and hard work from editing documents which previously would be handwritten. Text can be changed easily, saved in different forms so that children can compare one version with another and select the one they feel is best. This elementary aspect of word-processing is practised in many schools; however, often the work is lost. Children are not taught to save documents to a folder. Regular saving should be taught from the outset (Anderson, 2005). This in itself is a skill children need to know. It helps if they are coached in the practice of inserting the file path at the bottom of the page, which helps them find the document in future. Naming folders is also a skill which is especially important when several children are using the same machine. Saving the folder to the desktop can help them in locating it again rather than having to trawl though several pathways. However, children should be taught at a later stage to save to folders within files rather than the desktop as continual saving to the desktop will eventually clutter the desktop. Teaching children into using a flash or pen drive and keeping their work, particularly in the latter stages of Key Stage 2, is important and prepares them for life at secondary level. TextHELP™ is a program designed to help in the construction and editing of text and used by many support teachers. Each version improves on the last and you need to check on the suitability and functions of the version being used.

Dyslexic people who have difficulty with traditional typefaces may find relief by using a new typeface. This typeface may encompass simpler forms of letters and greater spacing between some letters which may otherwise merge or appear similar, letters such as *c* and *e*. The letters may be designed to have their own shape rather than be just a mirror image of another. The *b* in this typeface has no lower angle, rather a single sweeping curve up to the upright of the letter, whereas the *d* is the same as this typeface and has the sharp angle at the bottom. This helps readers and writers to know the difference between the two letters. More information can be gained from the website.

Editing text

Writing using the computer is one of the main tools for all children as the lack of permanence afforded by paper-based versions is encouraging for children who at the click of a button can change text without the need for tedious rewriting. The editing feature of word-processing programs is the main usefulness for most dyslexic children, but it can also prove the most frustrating as they can delete whole swathes of text with the simple click of a button. Highlighting and using the Relocate feature can cause untold misery if the highlighted text is not deselected before using the backspace key for other purposes, as this will delete all the text highlighted. Similarly, delete and backspace can cause frustration as using the backspace deletes the previous text while the delete button deletes ahead of the cursor.

The Insert button is similarly frustrating as this will then activate the function of all text being typed replacing the existing text. Pressing the Insert key again will deactivate this function.

'Drag and drop' features and 'copy and paste' are useful functions but can be difficult for children with motor control problems and need considerable practice for the function to be used efficiently. The use of the 'undo' function in the 'edit' tab is an important function to get used to. Exercises in completing this task, despite being tedious, can, in the end, produce a more practised and efficient user. The copy and paste facility needs to be used selectively and supervision of reading electronic texts needs to take account of the ease with which children can copy and paste whole chunks of text in information texts in much the same way that chunks were copied in paper-based versions, only with greater ease with electronic texts. Preparation for electronic reading and note-taking should include the use of a Word page and paper-based notes responding to specific questions rather than just copying and pasting most of an article into an identical document for marking by the teacher.

Using word-processing as part of the literacy session can include children with learning difficulties in the main part of the lesson, and Medwell et al. (2007b) provide many suggestions of how to develop writing, including shared writing. They also provide guidance on reading electronic texts although the advice does tend to assume students are literate readers.

Spellchecking is a skill that needs specific teaching. Many spellcheckers will not automatically select the most sensible word when a word is misspelled to such an extent that the spellchecker does not recognise it. This is when phonics can be brought to bear on the task; the child has to read the words suggested and decide which one, if any, is the one required. They need to understand that sometimes the word required is not in the list and they need to ask for help or resort to other more traditional forms of research such as the Awful Spellers Dictionary. Anderson notes that the option of 'ignore' is very close to 'change', and 'add' and 'suggest' are also close together. It is very easy for the child to misunderstand the commands as well, with a child using the 'add' button thinking they are adding the correct spelling to the text, rather than the 'change' button. This adds the incorrect spelling to the dictionary rather than correcting the text. The custom dictionary should be checked regularly for discrepant spellings (Anderson, 2005).

Using the mouse

The mouse on all machines is set to default of right-handedness. This needs to be changed for left-handed pupils so that the functions on the buttons are reversed. This can be achieved by accessing Control Panel and Mouse. Similarly, for all pupils the size of the pointer can be enlarged, as the standard size of the pointer is difficult to see for many dyslexic children. It is also possible to select numeric keys on the keypad to control the mouse pointer. Mouse skills can be improved by the playing of games which often come preloaded with typing tutor programs.

One word of caution: when you have shown pupils how to change formats and personal preferences, children may well investigate the possibilities themselves with sometimes unfortunate results. One child made the whole screen go blank by changing the font colour to white, the same as the background colour.

Keyboard

The layout of the keyboard is set and I have not seen a keyboard with the keys laid out in mirror image. It is possible to get an alphabetical keyboard rather than the standard qwerty keyboard; however, this has little advantage over the traditional one. If children are experiencing difficulty with a keyboard it is possible to assign shortcuts to keys in order to insert whole words. This is similar to the concept keyboard and while it can be useful in the early stages, stores problems for later when a child has to revert to the normal keyboard. What is possible is to acquire either a capital-letter keyboard or an enlarged keyboard for early use while the child is getting used to the location of the keys. The pressure of different keyboards can be challenging and again you can purchase very sensitive keyboards which will respond to the pressure of a puff of air from a 'blower'. Sensitive keyboards can be acquired from speciality stockists. Overly sensitive keyboards, though, can pose their own problems in responding to the least touch by adding nonsense to the text.

Organisation of the desktop

One of the difficulties dyslexic children have is in finding the program needed from the Menu. Creating shortcuts can help with this but these then add clutter to the desktop. Selecting the most-often-used programs and grouping them on different parts of the desktop can help, as can changing the size of font so that they are more easily seen. The desktop background is also crucial as many icons can be lost against a busy background. Plain dark blue with yellow or pink icons is the best display. Folders can also be stored on the desktop and this encourages children to use folders.

Changing the size of font can assist in reading the desktop icons but if selected at too large a font can actually have the effect of some of the icons and titles 'dropping off' the edge of the page. You really need to play around with this until you have found the right size and layout for your pupils. If several pupils are using the same machine, having different 'log on' accounts will automatically select their personal settings.

Computer games

There are many games available on the computer which can be used to practise mathematics and spelling. These are readily available from many sites when you undertake a simple Google search. The disadvantage of these sites is they are not designed for your particular pupils. It is relatively simple to develop your own games or programs using PowerPoint and even a simple game which is specific to your pupil(s) will be better than a more complicated one which is irrelevant to your pupils.

You can also purchase some games which allow you to adapt the content. Programs such as Lexis™, which is designed for dyslexic pupils and allows you to select the difficulty level and content from a selection, are ideal.

If you are using computer games, remember that they need supervision, as much as, if not more so, than other games. Children may give up because they keep going around in a loop without completing the game or they may complete it through trial and error rather than from understanding. You need to be close by to discuss how the game is proceeding and check on progress.

Commercial computer games which are freely available and which many children will have at home are not without their virtues either. These games can teach mouse control or fine motor control using the joy stick, etc. They can hone co-ordination and with some games aid the tracking of objects which all help with sub-reading skills.

Caution should be used when accessing web-based games. Some of these are very tedious and can be just as demotivating as poorly-designed board games. You need to access these games yourself, test them out and evaluate them before allowing your pupils to play with them.

Video conferencing

Video conferencing is a valuable tool for children and one they may well be familiar with from home, where many children use a well-known program to talk to friends online using a web camera at the same time.

There are certain procedures which need to be taught for good video conferencing. These customs are not usual or necessary with face-to-face talk because of the immediate contact. Using video conferencing, children need to be aware that you need to face the camera and to stay within the focus area of the camera; it is quite strange talking to someone who suddenly disappears off camera, and talking in turn is especially important with video. Other habits which it may be assumed go unnoticed because the person is not with you need to be drawn to attention also. It is not uncommon for children to pick their nose while on video conferencing – because the person is not next to them, they don't realise that every movement is observed from afar.

The time lapse with some video conferences can be a little disconcerting, too, and children need to be aware of the need for patience in allowing for this time delay.

Thinking beyond the obvious

Mention ICT and most teachers will probably think of computers; some may include voice recorders, digital cameras, TV or programmable resources such as the Roamer. Few will think about mobile phones, pagers, walkie-talkies, other programmable toys or the opportunities afforded by texting. Many will not include the use of email when using computers yet these are the very tools children will be using in their everyday lives. Many primary age children will already be using social sites to upload information and pictures of themselves or even video chat with their friends. Some may even have their own web space by the age of 11. Often these sources of ICT are ignored.

2 TXT or not?

Spelling or the lack of it which goes with text messaging and emails is often a concern in the teaching of English. With pupils who are dyslexic it could be viewed as a positive advantage. No one spells 'correctly' in text messaging although there are accepted conventions within the system such as the mixed use of numbers and letters to create words such as 'l8r' and the use of single letters to stand for whole words such as in 'c u' in place of 'see you'. This sort of creative spelling can free many dyslexic children from the chains and constraints of normal spelling and allow them to communicate freely. Imagine being able to write exactly what you want without the worry of how to spell it because no one spells correctly anyway! This is a wonderful opportunity not to be missed in teaching dyslexic pupils. As long as the differences between the two media are drawn to the attention of pupils so that they know of the appropriateness of using such abbreviations then you are empowering them as communicating people rather than teaching them incorrect spellings. Indeed, by purposely using incorrect spellings you are drawing their attention to this form as a distinct form as well as the correct form. Predictive text is a useful tool; however, children also need to know how to turn predictive text off and how to insert their own particular word.

Teaching the use of the function keys may be unnecessary as many children will have already overtaken adults in this knowledge; but if they do not know it then you should check they know how to use the Insert whole word, Insert numbers, Use predictive text, etc. There is also the challenge that many phone companies differ from each other in this aspect.

Note of caution

Many schools ban the use of mobile phones in school and even collect them when pupils arrive. It may be necessary to change the thinking of the literacy subject leader or head teacher on this matter. As a student teacher you are in the unique position of being able to ask to carry out research on this aspect as part of your course. Many head teachers are loathe to obstruct the course of knowledge and research and will agree. When they see the results you may be able to influence future practice.

Digital cameras

Digital cameras have a wealth of use for children, especially pupils with dyslexia who either have difficulty with remembering sequences or cannot think of anything to say. Using a digital camera to record an event and then sequencing the shots is a powerful tool for helping children to organise their thoughts. Many digital cameras also have a voice-record facility for shots, which allows children to put a short reminder on the memory card of what the shot is about. Video is also available on many digital cameras and allows children to take short films of up to around 30 minutes, depending on the capacity of the memory card.

Using photographic stimulus often changes how children record and use grammar. Many children when looking at photographs of what they have been doing, such as baking, will use the present tense to outline what is happening in the photos. This is an aspect which can be capitalised on when teaching different tenses.

Summary of key difficulties of using ICT

- Inability to type at speed.
- Slow construction of language.
- Bizarre spellings.
- Cannot use spell-checker properly.
- Uses spell-checker incorrectly and adds incorrect spellings to the dictionary.
- Cannot file a document.
- If a document is filed, cannot retrieve it.
- Cannot read on-screen menu.
- Cannot retain instructions in the memory.
- Poor mouse control.
- Cannot flip between screens.
- Cannot operate machinery that requires several stages to make it work.
- Cannot read manual.
- Cannot repeat a process they have discovered through trial and error.
- Cannot remember how to operate programs when shown how.
- Often pushed off ICT equipment because of slowness.

Key principles for using ICT

- Touch-typing needs to be taught early on. This is time-consuming but is the technological equivalent to teaching handwriting.
- Hardware has to be adaptable to the needs of groups of pupils and individuals.

- Instructions have to be ready and easily followed and allow pupils independence.
- Accessibility is a key aspect which schools need to be aware of.
- ICT should be used as often as possible in as many lessons as possible so that the pupil becomes familiar with it.
- Teaching assistants and teachers need to be familiar with the programs, what might go wrong and how to quickly remedy the situation.

CASE STUDY

We left Jack in the case study in Chapter 5 wanting to word-process his work. Using computers was something that only the most able children did because they finished first. Word-processing was seen as a reward and final stage of the writing process. The class had ICT lessons once a week in the computing suite but the pace was such that many children were left behind and only a few could remember from week to week what they had learnt. This is a situation replicated in many classrooms around Britain.

Jack had remarkably good co-ordination skills because he spent many hours at home playing computer games, he had good mouse skills and could use the certain shortcut keys on the keyboard quickly. Unfortunately, he had also picked up one-finger typing. I would like to report that Jack made wonderful progress using the computer but this would be untrue. Jack did word-process his work but it was painfully slow and was only finished by taking turns with another child who could type with accuracy and speed. This did have a positive side, though. Jack realised that *he* had to be able to read his work or *someone else* did in order to word-process it. It also gave him contact with children who were achieving at a higher level than he was. This had a positive effect on his self-esteem because he would not normally have been partnered with such children. Jack really needed to go back to basics and learn to use the keyboard with accuracy and speed, otherwise the difficulty he had with handwriting was just replicated in the use of technology. A concept keyboard would have been one solution for Jack but his oral language outstripped basic vocabulary suitable for a concept keyboard. When I last saw Jack he had overcome some of his reluctance to write but he was still struggling with the mechanics of writing and word-processing. Ideally I would have liked to have worked with him a little longer and maybe introduced him to story-sequencing software, producing his own short action sequences. This was not to be though, and Jack started into Key Stage 2 having gained a lot of ground and made progress but still with a hill to climb ahead of him.

A SUMMARY OF **KEY POINTS**

> ICT should be integrated into lessons with specific tuition for certain skills.

> ICT includes not only computers but audio recording, visual recording and digital cameras; in mathematics it can also include programmable equipment such as the Roamer. You can locate many activities to use on the Roamer at www.kented.org.uk/ngfl/ict/roamer.htm. It should also include the use of internet resources and genuine research on the internet, not just reading Word documents on screen or writing Word documents.

> ICT is most useful when time has been taken to develop specific skills and when the child is focused on the task (history or English) rather than the keyboard.

> ICT needs to be valued as an alternative to written records and is equivalent to, not inferior to, written work.

MOVING *ON* > > > **> > >** MOVING *ON* > > > **> > >** MOVING *ON*

Examine how computers and other ICT equipment are used in your school. Look in cupboards to see what is hidden away.

Examine curriculum documents to see where ICT is mentioned; plot ICT documentation against core documents.

REFERENCES REFERENCES **REFERENCES** REFERENCES **REFERENCES** REFERENCES

Anderson, B (2005) *Using computers with SpLD students.* Information sheet 6, Patoss, www.green wold.freeserve.co.uk/6computers.htm (accessed on 3/2/2005)

Anderson, R (2007) *Dyslexia and inclusion: supporting classroom reading with 7–11-year-olds.* Leicester: UKLA minibook 26

Bearne, E, Clark, C, Johnson, A, Manford, P, Mottram, M, Wolstencroft, H, Anderson, R, Gamble, N and Overall, L (2007) *Reading on screen.* Leicester: UKLA

Butteriss, S and Litterick, I (2008) Mobile technology to help the dyslexic learner, in *The Dylsexia Handbook 2008/9.* Bracknell: The British Dyslexia Association

Crivelli, V (2008) Using existing and new technology to support dyslexic children, in *The Dyslexia Handbook 2008/9.* Bracknell: British Dyslexia Association

Medwell, J, Moore, G, Wray, D and Griffiths, V (2007a) *Primary English hnowledge and understanding.* Exeter: Learning Matters

Medwell, J, Wray, D, Coates, E, Minns, H and Griffiths, V (2007b) *Primary English teaching theory and practice.* Exeter: Learning Matters

Ofsted (1999) *Pupils with specific learning difficulties in mainstream schools.* London: HMSO

Useful websites

textHELP is available from ianSYST Ltd, www.dyslexic.com

or

textHELP systems, Enkalon Business Centre, 25 Randalstown Road, Antrim, N. Ireland BT41 4LJ. www.texthelp.com

read regular, www.readregular.com/english/intro.html (accessed 27/8/08)

Roamer, www.kented.org.uk/ngfl/ict/roamer.htm

Further help and ideas
www.primaryresources.co.uk/ict/roamer.htm
www.ictcentre.wiltslea.org.uk/sen.htm
partners.becta.org.uk/page_documents/research/wtrs_ictsupport.pdf
www.icteachers.co.uk/teachers/links/tsen.htm

9
Conclusion

Chapter objectives

By the end of this chapter you should be aware of:

- **the learning potential of using games;**
- **how the different aspects of teaching English are interrelated;**
- **how putting fun back into teaching achieves a better outcome than providing tired and 'dry' activities;**
- **using games is in line with current thinking about emotional intelligence.**

Introduction

REFLECTIVE TASK

Why use games?

Write down ten reasons why a teacher should use games.

Justification and the place of games

A message from the Head of the QCA

Schools that are providing an inspiring and challenging curriculum look not only at the subject requirements but also at the development of the underlying skills, qualities and competencies; the skills that contribute to life-long learning. Above all, these schools engage their pupils in an open-ended, investigative approach to learning where pupils' interest is engaged, where there is a sense of purpose and relevance, where pupils are active, where new ideas are explored, and where learning is fun.

(Mick Waters, Director of Curriculum, QCA, 2006)

This focus on fun has resurrected creativity, and it is creativity you need to bring to your teaching. Creativity allows you to deviate from the constricting plans that are used in many schools but which should be used as a framework rather than a straitjacket.

Games provide the practice and motivation for children to learn. It is important to understand some of the ways children learn and to present you with an ideology for learning and teaching. Children can learn in different ways and have done throughout history according to the prevailing ideology. Children can learn through experimentation and play in programmes such as Montessori (Montessori, 1994; Gettman, 1995; Montessori and Hunt, 2005), children can also learn through fear and brutality – however, this learning is likely to be short-lived and not transferable afterwards (Curran, 2008). Children can learn from peers and from adults with whom they share a particular bond or regard. It is this regard and respect for the ways children learn as unique individuals and their right to learn in a way that is meaningful and fun for them which is at the heart of this book. As Curran (2008) states: *If you have made good emotional connection with the person who is trying to learn from you (or from whom you are trying to learn) you have dramatically increased the chance of them learning that thing from you*. Emotional connection here is not about gushing love but about regard and respect for other people's security of mind, about reducing stress in learning about thinking *I can do this because this other person has faith in me.* Curran (2008) states that *emotions and emotional brains underpin everything we learn:*

> *Understand the human in front of you. Then you will improve their self esteem. If you do this you will improve their SELF CONFIDENCE. And if you do that, they will feel emotionally ENGAGED with what you are doing.*

> (Curran, 2008, pp81–2)

The philosophy of this book has been to leave behind the resources and techniques that have been used and failed with children with dyslexia and turn to what they naturally engage with, to reconnect with them and value their ability in playing games and to develop that natural competitiveness which emerges in games but is so often dismissed by the children themselves through worksheets, etc. Too often they have learnt that doing worksheets leaves them with low self-esteem because they cannot do them. It may also leave them with the effects of stress, something which until recently has been thought of as an adult complaint. Sustained stress in any age group depresses the release of dopamine (essential for normal and efficient brain functioning) and it also produces adrenalin and noradrenalin. These chemicals of the brain drive memory function into the unconscious part of the brain and can produce unwanted effects later on after the event, and finally stress can produce steroids in the body which kill cells in the hippocampus and amygdala. Curran (2008) asserts that *As the hippocampus is one of the two crucial structures in the memory and is particularly involved in conscious short-term memory, to destroy nerve cells in it when you are trying to learn does not win as a good survival trait* (p77). Games improve motivation, self-esteem and engage students' interest while also (surreptitiously) teaching. Playing games with children will have them wanting to come back to your sessions rather than groaning about the work. It will engender a 'can do' approach rather than a 'don't want to' approach. Because the children are using their brains more, it will also improve the functioning of the brain.

PRACTICAL TASK PRACTICAL TASK PRACTICAL TASK PRACTICAL TASK PRACTICAL TASK

Select a topic you have found difficult to learn or to teach. Devise a game which would encourage you to practise or learn aspects of this topic.

What are the key elements you need to keep focused on and practising this?

In the previous chapters you have read not only the theoretical background to many aspects of dyslexia. You have also been reading about how to engage children's attention, how to devise activities which will enthuse them and which children will want to come back to. There are many aspects we have not covered, such as science, history, geography. This is not because you cannot apply the same principles to these subjects but rather because the constraints of this book dictate that the focus is on the subjects dyslexic pupils have most difficulty with. Your task now is to apply what you have learnt in the foregoing chapters to other subjects. One of the best history lessons I have seen was one where a student sent different letters to groups in the class containing information about life on board a boat in the eighteenth century. Half the class had letters and half had to go around interviewing those with letters, putting together the information in the letters to gain information about life on board at that time. The class were so enthused by this activity they did not realise they were learning, not only about history but developing and practising research skills as well as social skills of interviewing, etc. They were having fun.

Using games is an ideal way to teach and assess aspects of English and mathematics. Children are keen to participate, they are often competitive and therefore perform to their best ability. The challenge of using games is not so much in the games themselves but in the recording of the process and outcome, and in justifying their use to the less initiated who believe the only way to teach children is to sit them down and get them to complete a worksheet or write an account of something. This is something you will need to take account of and use ICT to record both the activity and the outcome. You will need to be an ambassador for active learning of this sort, even to the end of Key Stage 2. The use of a video camera can become normal practice in many classrooms and should not impede normal practice once children are used to it. Lack of formal recording is not a valid reason for abandoning games when it can be seen they support and promote learning so effectively. Formal recording is for the benefit of accountability, not for the benefit of the child.

Games are ideal for cross-curricular work, an aspect of planning which is becoming more popular. They also fit in with the agenda for learning styles and teaching and learning strategies rather than subject sessions. They can easily take account of the different intelligences put forward by Gardner.

Games are open to adaptation to individual styles according to learning preference as long as they are kept open as suggested throughout this book. Instructions can be given on tape through the use of a tape-recorder symbol on a board game. Some games can be totally auditory rather than card- or board-based.

This book has outlined the importance of involving key personnel in the education of children, including teaching assistants and parents. There are other personnel who may be called on for advice and support including advisory teachers, professional associations, LA staff and local higher educational institution staff who will offer support. Some will come into schools and work alongside teachers, devising teaching plans and adapting existing plans while looking at the needs of the child.

Do beware of free teaching plans and resources or the 'one size fits all' plans which are available from QCA. These are only guidance and should be modified for all children, more especially for children with learning disabilities.

Checklist

- What do I know now about dyslexia that I did not know before reading this book?
- What are the markers of the different subgroups of dyslexia?
- What resources would I now automatically consider essential when teaching dyslexic children?
- What resources would I need to teach each of the subgroups?
- Do I know how to manage my teaching assistant to best support all children in the class?
- Who are the key personnel in teaching dyslexic children?
- At what point do I need to work with the parents?
- At what point do I need to seek the advice of the SENCo?

MOVING *ON* > > > > > > MOVING *ON* > > > > > > MOVING *ON*

As I stated at the beginning of this book, if you take the games and activities from this book and make them your own, adapt them for the interests and abilities of your children, I will have succeeded in my aim. I urge you now to develop your own games, to look at the children in front of you and to ask yourself *if these were my children, how would I want them to be taught?* Engage the interest and motivation of your pupils and you will be well on the way to helping them learn; adapt your material to their needs and you will be three-quarters there; the remaining quarter is knowing your subject and for that you really do need to get down to the work of reading around the theory of how children learn to read, write and spell and how dyslexic children may be different. Use the recommended texts to follow up on this so that you make yourself your own expert.

REFERENCES REFERENCES **REFERENCES** REFERENCES **REFERENCES** REFERENCES

Curran, A (2008) *The LITTLE BOOK of BIG STUFF ABOUT the BRAIN*. Camarthen: Crown House Publishing

Waters, M (2006) A Message from the Head of the QCA. www.independentthinking.co.uk/Cool+Stuff/Hot+Tips/428.aspx (accessed 30/8/08)

Gettman, D (1995) *Basic Montessori*. Oxford: ABC-CLIO Ltd

Montessori, M (1994) *Discovery of the child*. New York: Random House

Montessori, M and Hunt, J (2005) *The Montessori method*. CA, USA: Kessinger Publishing

FURTHER READING FURTHER READING **FURTHER READING** FURTHER READING

Chinn, S (1998) *Sum hope. Breaking the numbers barrier*. London: Souvenir Press

Dias, K and Juniper, L (2002) Phono-graphix – who needs additional literacy support? An outline of research in Bristol schools. *Support for Learning*, 17 (1), NASEN

Fawcett, A (2002) Reading remediation: an evaluation of traditional phonologically-based interventions. A review for the Department for Education and Skills, the British Dyslexia Association and the Dyslexia Institute. *Review*, 3 March 2002

Ellis, S (2006) Open dialogue peer review. A response to Stuart. *The Psychology of Education Review*. 30 (2), September 2006

Goswami, U (2006) Open dialogue peer review: research evidence and teaching theories: a response to Stuart. *The Psychology of Education Review*, 30 (2), September 2006

Henson, R (2001) Serial order in short-term memory. *The Psychologist*, 14 (2), February 2001

Hickmott, O and Bendefy, A (2006) *Seeing spells achieving*. Buckingham: MX Publishing

Hook, P and Jones, S (2002) The importance of automaticity and fluency for efficient reading comprehension. *Perspectives*, Winter 2002: 9–14

Hornsby, B (1989) *Before alpha learning games for the under fives*. London: Souvenir Press

Hornsby, B (1995) *Overcoming dyslexia. A straightforward guide for families and teachers*. London: Vermillion

Hornsby, B (1999) *Alpha to Omega (5th edn)*. Oxford: Heinemann

Ofsted (2008) *Responding to the 'Rose Review': schools' approaches to the systematic teaching of phonics*. Reference no. 080038

Wearmouth, J (ed.) (2001) *Special educational provision in the context of inclusion policy and practice in schools*. London: David Fulton

Useful websites

Making the connection www.DyslexiaA2Z.com

Dyslexia and memory. Can it be helped by learning memory strategies? www.dyslexia-parent.com/mag39.htm

Interventions for students with learning disabilities. NICHCY *News Digest* Vol. 25 August 1997 www.ldonline.org/ld_indepth/teaching_technologies/nichcy_ibnterventions.html

American Hyperlexia Association www.hyperlexia.org/contents.html

Computers offer possible therapy for dyslexia http://chronicillnet.org/dyslexia.html

Glossary

ADHD Attention deficit hyperactivity disorder

AEN Additional educational needs

Aims What you as a teacher hope to provide for the children in an activity

BDA British Dyslexia Association

CoP Code of Practice

DCSF Department for Children, Schools and Families

DfEE Department for Education and Employment

DfES Department for Education and Skills

EHRC Equalities and Human Rights Commission

HEI Higher Education Institution

IBP Individual Behaviour Plan

IEP Individual Education Plan

ITT Initial Teacher Training

IWB Interactive whiteboard

LA Local (Education) Authority

Learning outcomes/objectives What the child should learn from undertaking the activity

NC National Curriculum

NLS National Literacy Strategy

NQT Newly qualified teacher

Ofsted Office for Standards in Education

PPA Planning preparation and Assessment

PNS Primary National Strategy

QCA Qualifications and Curriculum Authority

QTS Qualified Teacher Status

SEN Special educational needs

SENCo Special educational needs co-ordinator

SpLD Specific learning difficulties

TA Teaching assistant

Note: the letter 'i' after a page number refers to an illustration.